To Deborah Crosby
Best Wishes
and
Enjoy -

Charlotte Moss
1991

A
PASSION
FOR
DETAIL

DOUBLEDAY

New York   London   Toronto   Sydney   Auckland

CHARLOTTE MOSS

A PASSION FOR DETAIL

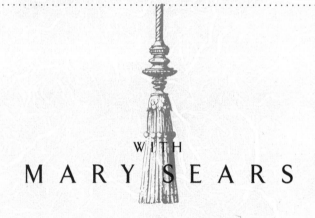

WITH
MARY SEARS

PHOTOGRAPHED BY
JOE STANDART

ILLUSTRATED BY
JIM STEINMEYER

Charlotte Moss

PUBLISHED BY DOUBLEDAY
a division of Bantam Doubleday Dell Publishing Group, Inc.
666 Fifth Avenue, New York, New York 10103

DOUBLEDAY and the portrayal of an anchor with a dolphin
are trademarks of Doubleday,
a division of Bantam Doubleday Dell Publishing Group, Inc.

Library of Congress Cataloging-in-Publication Data
Moss, Charlotte.
A passion for detail / Charlotte Moss with Mary Sears;
photographed by Joe Standart; illustrated by Jim Steinmeyer.—1st ed.
p.   cm.
1. Interior decoration accessories.   I. Sears, Mary.   II. Title.
NK2115.5.A25M67   1991   90-49975
747'.9—dc20   CIP
ISBN 0-385-26760-6

BOOK DESIGN BY CAROL MALCOLM-RUSSO
WITH GREGG SEVASTA

To my Mom

MARTHA CLAIRE MOSS

1927–1990

My mother's brother, Gene, said of her that "she elevated home-making to an art form." Gene's comment expresses in a few words the impact that my mother's care for life at home has had on me and how it has helped to shape my life. It is out of gratitude for this and countless other ways that she contributed to my growth that I dedicate my first book to her.

ACKNOWLEDGMENTS

Books of this nature rely on visuals to convey their message. For the visuals here I thank Joe Standart, my photographer, for his patience, professionalism, and of course, his wonderful photographs. I must say that we also had a good time, and when I got frustrated Joe kept smiling and cracking jokes until we got it right.

For the illustrations I thank Jimmy Steinmeyer, whose work is just the best I know, and who is an absolute delight to work with.

For the writing of this book Mary Sears first had to endure the hardship of interpreting my handwriting. Mary made sense of piles of notes written on pieces of paper, 5 × 8 cards, and the like, when most people would have given up. All of those Sundays in the office I faxed Mary page upon page, thinking she wouldn't be there to receive the heap—but lo and behold, at the end of my transmission I would receive a fax back—"Good night, Charlotte"—and then I knew it was time to quit.

Photographs are taken of houses and it is the owners of these houses that I wish to thank for allowing us to invade their homes. They were terrific sports. Michael and Sue Bloomberg, David Easton and Jimmy Steinmeyer, Nick and Clare Potter, Tom and Jordan Saunders, and John and Laura Pomerantz.

I also wish to thank . . .
Clinton, Joe's wife, for juggling the schedule and for being so understanding when he was late for dinner.

Diana Auchincloss for researching, organizing, and booking photography dates. Not to mention finding the files I always seemed to misplace, and faxing, faxing, faxing.

Marguerite Sellian for faxing page after page to Mary Sears, and for the patience necessary to do it.

Connie Newberry and Megan Ziglar, who ran the business in my absence and now have grown accustomed to doing it even when I'm there!

Patsy Corbin, my mentor and friend, who took me to lunch with Nancy Evans and made this book happen. Throughout the writing of this book Patsy continued to be my "kick in the pants."

Nancy Evans, whose vision, energy, and brains I greatly admire.

John Duff, my editor, who provided constructive criticism until it hurt, but without it I would probably still be doing rewrites. John's encouragement, faith, and ideas are woven throughout.

Phyllis Wender, my agent, whose support was limitless. She is my guardian angel.

Paul Bott and the staff at Twigs for the perfect flowers when we needed them, finding specific flowers when I wanted them, and being able to interpret with flowers the message I was trying to convey.

Valerie Winters, who manages my house, for the numerous lunches she prepared for our crew, and for taking care of *everything* at home while I was working.

My husband, Barry, and stepsons, James and Ben, for excusing me early from the table so I could go work, for forgiving my absences, and for their encouragement; they have been my cheering squad.

C O N T E N T S

...it is the result of a universal impulse to express the things of the spirit in visible form, the divine urge (or its devilish perversion) that sets mankind apart from his fellow creatures...

Its personality should express your personality, just as every gesture you make—or fail to make—expresses your gay animation or your restraint...

What is needed is a sense of domesticity...a feeling of privacy... an atmosphere of coziness..."

A
PASSION
FOR
DETAIL

INTRODUCTION

WHY

WE DECORATE

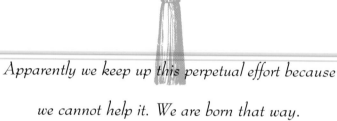

Apparently we keep up this perpetual effort because

we cannot help it. We are born that way.

Fundamentally, it is the result of a universal impulse

to express the things of the spirit in visible form,

the divine urge (or its devilish perversion) that sets

mankind apart from his fellow creatures

on this earth and denies him their peaceful existence.

Sarah M. Lockwood,
Decoration: Past, Present,
and Future

W*HEN I SET OUT TO WRITE THIS* book, I was overwhelmed with ideas that I wanted to share. Since making interior design my career (and indeed, as you'll discover, I've been "decorating" all my life), I've experienced the pleasure and the pitfalls that come with "dressing up" the places where people live.

A few truths have unfolded in the process.

The first is this: everyone has their own personal style. The idea, in decorating, is to teach your house your own language. There's a knack to it, and once mastered, you'll never forget it. In a sense it's another language we all learn, to one degree or another. I think the houses I've chosen for the book are all owned by people who are fluent in the language of decorating. And you know what happens when you spend some time with those who speak the language—you get fluent, too! Then your house expresses *you*.

We've all experienced houses like this—a house that lets the voices of its owners be heard. When a house speaks, you can walk in and see and hear, smell and touch, the echoes of many lives— even when (sometimes, especially when!) no one is home.

If you've ever done any house-sitting, you'll know what I mean. Without a personality to light up a room, you're left with the footstools, the flowers, and the table linens to tell a story all their own—and tell they do!

Which brings us to my second point: people's lives are expressed in little details. The pocket handkerchief, the colored paper clip, the silver compact—all are telling gestures that proclaim who we are. And nowhere is this more apparent than in decorating. The soap in the bathroom, the flowers in the garden, the books on the bedside table are all strong symbols of a life in progress. You look at these details and a world unfolds—here are their books, the paintings they cherish, the music that soothes their souls.

Decorating—and accessorizing in particular—is one of the most personal activities we can pursue. It is a form of self-expression.

There are no formulas, no special magic, no right or wrong way. Just what is right for you.

The third truth I discovered is that houses never truly sing until personal style unfolds. The best houses have "come out of their cocoons"—the cocoons of decorating rules, do's and don'ts, what's right and what's wrong. Who doesn't hold a memory of at least one special house that was so real, so tactile, so comforting, that its details remain in memory many years later, and sometimes long after the actual house has been dismantled or redone?

Every building, every house, every room tells a story about life as it was or is lived. We spend the majority of our lives within these spaces. Therefore, it only makes sense that they should mirror our tastes, values, personality, and the quality of the lives we lead.

Because I have a passion for history, many of the homes that have made an impression on me are those I've read about in books or biographies. The people who fascinate me—people such as Thomas Jefferson, Coco Chanel, and Fred Astaire—are a mixed bag, to be sure, but they all have a lot in common. A sense of humor, a gifted eye, a passion for detail, and style deep in their bones emerge as common themes among many. Their homes reflect personal choices and a personal vision.

I've included homes from the pages of history throughout the book. I hope they will encourage you to seek or refine your own style—with humor, with passion, and with love. Perhaps you'll pick up a new way of doing something by seeing someone else's example.

That's why we read decorating magazines and books such as this one, isn't it? Maybe you'll turn Grandma's vase into a lamp. Maybe you'll use a treasured porcelain compote as a place for potpourri. Maybe you'll pull your tea set out from under wraps. Or display your collection of clay circus animals. Or line up your wooden Noah's Ark on your bookshelf. In other words, let yourself show!

I often feel like a detective—a sleuth—when I walk into a house for the first time. It has a scent, an atmosphere as telling as perfume, as clear as a bold signature on the wall. And that signature tells a lot about the people who live here.

The same instinct has me peering closely at pictures in decorating magazines, straining to see the titles of the books on the shelves, the names of the magazines on the table. The idea being: what do they read/who are they?

When looking at the best historical rooms, the same holds true. Although the occupants no longer live, they live on in the rooms they have left behind. A close look reveals that someone actually lived in these rooms, built a life here, tackled family concerns, and celebrated joyous occasions within their walls. And by taking a broader view, solutions to your own decorating problems may come to light in ways you hadn't expected.

So come along. I have tried to shape for you a book that will delight the eye, arouse your senses and your curiosity, make you smile, scratch your head, confirm what you already know, instill some confidence, and get you organized. But, above all, I hope this book will make you look at your own house from a new perspective —a perspective that I hope will be infinitely more relaxed. If any one or combination of the above is achieved, I will feel I have accomplished my mission.

Charlotte Moss

I

DEVELOPING YOUR
OWN PERSONAL
STYLE

Its personality should express your personality,

just as every gesture you make—or fail to make—

expresses your gay animation or your restraint,

your old fashioned conventions, your perplexing mystery,

or your emancipated modernism—

whichever characteristics are typically yours.

Emily Post, *The Personality
of the House,* 1930

S *IX YEARS AGO I SPOKE A DIFFERENT* language—one that included limited part-nerships, options, and arbitrage.

Now I speak a new language. It's the "at home" language of design and decoration.

Putting things together is what it's all about.

Selecting and placing decorative items in the home is a highly personal process. What we select for our walls, tabletops, bookshelves, mantels, bedside tables, or coffee tables says who we are.

Your house should have your stamp. When you hear people say that your house looks like you, you should feel you have succeeded. In a successful room, personality triumphs over decoration.

We learn to do things step by step. When I was little, my training wheels helped me gain confidence before advancing to a two-wheeler. When I learned to swim I knew the water was only a few feet deep. Knowing I could touch bottom with my head still above water gave me confidence. Practicing an oral book report in front of a mirror gave me confidence, and turning on the stereo and dancing alone in my room before the "big dance" helped give me confidence, too.

You see, practice may not make perfect, but it definitely helps make us more relaxed and confident in our pursuit. If you are to be original in your approach to anything, you must not follow rules established by some arbitrary source.

The principles I am about to lay out for you are not rules on the best way to hang pictures over a sofa or the best way to arrange objects on a mantelpiece. Instead, I give you the "Moss Rules." I

Photograph on previous page

This elegant spot by the window is a certain draw for anyone intent on conversation. The velvet love seat with needlepoint pillow and the delicately fringed lampshade set an intimate tone. Two gilt chairs can easily be drawn into the dialogue. A quartet of animal paintings, two Chinese export plates, and a pair of "dummy-board" tole mantel garnitures painted with figures in nineteenth-century costume provide their share of lightness and balance.

have found these rules quite useful, and they have formed the outline of many of the lectures.

These rules—suggestions, if you will—have been embellished by me over the years, but one guiding light is something my dad said to me years ago: "Observing doesn't cost a dime." He is a great believer in researching before purchasing, and doing one's homework by completely knowing the market. Dad also said, "Always keep your sense of humor."

I am a firm believer in doing homework. You will be way ahead of the game if you accept the notion that homework is essential—yes, even as an adult.

People have asked me many times, how did I know what to buy, and where to buy it, when I opened my shop? How could I leave banking and know exactly what I wanted to do and how to do it? Well, that was the easy part for me. For years I have been a researcher, a clipper, a note-taker, a file keeper, ad nauseum. As a child, as a teenager, and in my adult life, I have always enjoyed the hunt. Flea markets, auctions, wrecking companies, junk shops, catalogues, magazines, books, museums, historic homes, and elegant antiques shops have also been part of my education, and will complete your own curriculum for a "Master's Degree in Details."

The "Moss Rules," or steps toward education of the eye, begin with *observing*. But it does not stop there. You must read. Clip. Visit. Take Notes. Keep Files. And, above all, trust yourself.

CECIL BEATON

1904–80

While perhaps best remembered for his photographs of the rich and royal, Cecil Beaton's talents went much farther than the camera's lens. A theatrical designer and author, Beaton possessed a most correct and noble mien. The social circles he traveled in found him rare and gifted indeed.

Through his voluminous personal diaries, we glimpse what it was like for him to furnish a new house—the charming Reddish House in Broadchalke, a small English village near London, where he lived from 1947 until his death in 1980.

The Queen Anne house, with its rambling, informal arrangement of rooms and steep garden in the back, appeared bleak and cheerless to Beaton at first visit. However, the next visit occurred on a sunnier day, and he was struck by the dignity and elegance of the place.

Beaton's drawing room was a stage set of sorts. The room was as theatrical as its occupant. The deep aubergine walls formed a moody backdrop which showed off his treasured objects from around the world. These large-scale surroundings were hardly surprising for the man with the photographer's eye who was used to decorating massive theater sets for the era's most luminous stars.

I'm for style—fashions change too often.
Coco Chanel

This sitting room designed by Jamie Drake is a multi-layered mix of texture and detail, and full of surprises for the eye. Yet the overall effect is soft and light. Furniture is arranged with the fireplace as a focal point, and instead of a cocktail table, a brocade-covered ottoman presides. The mirrored chimney breast is lit by a pair of Austrian sconces encrusted with delicately painted porcelain flowers. The ceiling, stippled in a soft sky-blue shade, echoes the tone of the silky striped curtains, with their bow-tied swags and jabots.

Whether you finished school some time ago or are still in school today, you cannot assume your education ends with graduation. You must design a special curriculum for yourself, just like the one I have suggested. If you are reading this book, you obviously have an interest in interior decoration. Why not try my "rules" and then embellish them or edit them as you go along? They will provide you with a solid foundation.

In literature, art, decoration, or business, the concept of observation is translatable. Flaubert's theory of observation was a great influence on the writings of Guy de Maupassant. In *Pierre and Jean*, de Maupassant says:

> *It is a matter of looking at anything you want to express long enough and closely enough to discover in it some aspect that nobody has yet seen or described . . . the most insignificant thing contains some little unknown element. We must find it.*

Georgia O'Keeffe, as quoted in Laurie Lisle's biography, *Portrait of an Artist,* translated this feeling in her own terms as it applied to her art:

> *Still—in a way—nobody sees a flower—really—it is so small—we haven't time . . . and to see takes time . . .*

To be a great writer one must observe people, and to be a great painter one must observe nature. In decoration, you might see iron grillwork patterns on a townhouse and think how they might be adapted as a fabric pattern, or notice a neoclassical stone frieze that might make a wonderful design to paint on a chest of drawers.

This is not to say, however, that everyone must *be* a great decorator. But in order to develop your own personal style, you must be aware of your surroundings.

Visit decorator showhouses. Read the showhouse journal and take notes on what you like. Keep the journal—there are great resources inside.

Attend auctions. Buy catalogues and request the sale report so you can record the hammer price.

Explore museums and buy exhibition catalogues. These catalogues are written by experts and provide excellent summaries of a style, a period, or the work of a single artist.

Scour flea markets. I love flea markets, junk shops, and estate sales. I know people who would never admit this. I know people who can't believe I shop at places like these.

In some of the most curious and unlikely places, I have found paintings, porcelains, linens, baskets, ribbon, antique fabric, great books, antique tole, and flower vases by the dozens.

The strategy of flea market shopping is simple, yet complex. If you go in search of a particular object your eye will "edit out" other very suitable objects. This method sets you up for disappointment.

However, if you go for the pleasure of it, for the mere hunt, you are bound to see something to come home with.

Don't forget that objects are not the only benefit to shopping a flea market. Your curiosity will be rewarded and you may come home with some great ideas—and the exhilaration is free!

Flowers are the inescapable theme in the house of artist Clare Potter and her husband, Nick. Summer, winter, rain or shine, the flowers bloom everywhere. Here in the living room, an eighteenth-century watercolor of tulips hangs from a moiré bow, surrounded by a plethora of Victorian watercolors.

An interior is the natural projection of the soul . . .
Coco Chanel

In the golden glow of the living room of Laura and John Pomerantz, one of a pair of carved pine corner cupboards show off favorite treasures: salt-glazed jugs, majolica plates, and French miniatures painted on ivory. Deep-red stripes on the damask sofa set off sparks against the warmth of the walls. The lamp base is made of turned granite and topped with a gold-covered shade.

READ, CLIP, AND KEEP FILES

I have files on every conceivable topic. I keep notebooks on rooms I like, drawings of curtain treatments, upholstered furniture, lamps and lampshades, etc., etc., etc.

Files line the bookcases behind my desk, I have "leased" some space in my husband's library, and I even have them under my bed and under my desk at home. I can't bear the thought of throwing anything away. Inevitably, if I do, I will need it the next day—even if I haven't referred to it for a year.

I keep files for cities that I visit. In between visits I throw in notes on shops, exhibitions, and people, and make a point of pursuing them when I arrive. Every visit *always* includes a new place, a new shop, or a new source of information or products.

After you have educated your eye by observing, reading, clipping, and visiting, you must now take the next and most difficult step. You must trust yourself. All of the accumulated knowledge in the world will be useless if you cannot trust yourself when it comes to selecting and arranging objects in your home. Personal style develops from knowledge and confidence—the confidence needed to take risks.

For centuries, people the world over have been concerned with the decoration and ultimate comfort of their environment. But it was not until early in this century that practitioners who called themselves "interior decorators" set up offices and collected fees for helping other people make their house a home.

[Taste] is an evolution and refinement of one's personal likes and dislikes. This evolution takes place with a constant curiosity and interest in everything. The editing consequently refines the choices and defines taste.

Norma Kamali, fashion designer

I hope this book will help you learn that in order to begin the process of decorating you must relax and forget all the silly rules you've read about or been told. Reexamine and reevaluate all the things that decorate your home. Trust yourself. Walk away, go out to lunch, come back, and take a fresh look. The longer we live with things a certain way in a certain location, the less we see them. Relocating objects can sometimes make a room take on a different meaning.

Some argue that personal style is innate. American fashion designer Bill Blass says, "Style is primarily a matter of instinct." And I have to agree.

The manner in which we develop our personal style varies with the individual. I know that in my own case the influence of my maternal grandmother, my mother, and my father, plus a high energy level and curiosity have pushed me to learn more about the things that interest me.

LASTING IMPRESSIONS

Of course, we all have lasting impressions that influence our homes and how we decorate them. Whether direct or indirect, these influences follow us throughout our lives.

I remember so well my grandmother's cottage on the Potomac River, with its deep red wicker furniture with floral printed cushions. Flowers were everywhere—on fabric, in pictures, on china, and in it.

"Woodrow Terrace," my grandmother's house in the city, was filled with pictures, bibelots, lace-draped tables, squashy comfortable chairs, and lots of books . . . the bathrooms were stocked with creams, lotions, and soaps of all shapes, colors, and fragrances. I loved spending the night there because she would let me stay in the bath forever.

She had a sun porch full of greenery, of plants that bloomed all year long according to the seasons; a lawn that sloped down toward a tree-lined street, and a driveway lined with pink crape myrtle that in the summer gave the illusion of a long pink tunnel leading to her house.

There were a pair of huge yew trees. I liked to sit underneath them and think. A hedge of purple bearded iris separated the front and back sections of the rear lawn. In early spring, the back lawn was a blanket of violets that led you to the doghouse where my grandfather's beagles, Romeo and Juliet, lived.

Periwinkle-colored hydrangeas greeted you at the front door along with the distinctive smell of my favorite shrub tree, boxwood.

I remember the comfortable, welcoming smell of the kitchen, where there was always something baking in the oven. In the musty attic I would hide for hours reading my mother's childhood scrapbooks and trying on my grandmother's hats and shoes from the twenties and thirties. My grandmother kept everything; I guess her attic was her diary.

Her reading interests ran to gardening journals, gardening

In the musty attic I would hide for hours . . . trying on my grandmother's hats and shoes from the twenties and thirties.

Jim Steinmeyer 1990

FRED ASTAIRE

1899–1987

Fred Astaire was perfection amid the satin sofas and cocktail shakers that comprised his on-screen life. Equally at ease with the simple tweeds and cottons that surrounded him in real life, Astaire's elegance didn't come from his surroundings. He carried his elegance with him.

Astaire professed to care nothing for clothes, but his long elegant silhouette is embedded in everyone's memory: the tie for a belt, the trademark gray flannels (a bit short, to show off his shoes). His daughter, Ava, recalls how he would rummage through the Beverly Hills dime store for just the right shiny bit of chain or rhinestone to brighten up his shoes or slippers.

Astaire's Beverly Hills home was as unpretentious as he was. Built in 1960, six years after the death of his first wife, Phyllis, the house reflects the tastes and passions of a gentleman living alone.

Astaire's library is as handsome and modest. A pool table and backgammon table beckoned willing comers. A grand portrait of his beloved racehorse Triplicate dominated one wall. There were plump chairs and a sofa for conversation. Another wall was entirely bookshelves, displaying Astaire's awards and a bird portrait by Irving Berlin. The furniture and fabrics were classic and well chosen, befitting this man of stature and grace.

Astaire was not much for excess, or for dwelling on frivolous things. "I don't think too much about my house," he once said, "I just enjoy it."

books, and current fiction. Her loyalties were to her family and her homes, her church and friends, and the garden club.

I truly believe, though we never discussed it, that she felt everyone should do their share to make this earth a better and prettier place. She certainly did.

I remember when she served one of her numerous luncheon buffets for children, grandchildren, and great-grandchildren. The table was always beautifully set, the cloth of lace or linen, perhaps one of the many she hand-embroidered.

She was a true homemaker. In addition, she worked for a number of years in the china department of a local department store.

If it is possible that the love of porcelain is inherited, then I acquired those genes from my grandmother.

She never taught me any rules—I'm not sure she followed any herself—but she did do one thing, and that was to teach me (through osmosis I guess) about color, balance, proportions, and appropriateness. Her credo was that I should always do the best with what I had.

I learned that an ordinary hand towel can be made extra special with a colorful border executed in the basic slip stitch. Or you could stitch your name or embroider your favorite flower.

My mother inherited many of these same qualities. Mom could make muslin look luxurious with the addition of trimmings. Her green thumb has always made me marvel. She can put anything in the ground and it will flourish.

When I was a teenager, Mom would always let me redecorate my room. Mind you, we did not go out and buy new furniture, but we would paint furniture, make new curtains, dust ruffles, and shams. (The bed covers were always something that were crocheted or quilted and who knows how old!) I remember the kidney-shaped dressing table for all of my treasures, souvenirs, and porcelains that came from my grandmother, family trips, gifts, or backyard sales. Mom was always very patient with me when I wanted to rearrange the living room furniture, too.

Of course, back then I lived there. I was a part of the house. Now, I would never walk into my mother's house and suggest something or move things around, but once asked—well—we would probably move furniture, hang pictures, look through magazines for more ideas, and we might even end up shopping for something.

I remember shopping at Montaldo's in Richmond, Virginia. Montaldo's was different from any other store. Their quiet gray-and-white decor and striped shopping bags appealed to me even at age thirteen. I was impressed at how something so pale and understated could be so stylish. I loved going downtown and buying my status symbol: Frank Cardone shoes with the tassels.

When I was thirteen, I got my first pair of Pappagallos—those little-more-than-ballet shoes that came in every conceivable color in which countless girls have sashayed across the floors of every country club in America.

When Pappagallos came into fashion (I use the term loosely), it was possible to "coordinate" your outfit from head to toe. The Bermuda bag allowed you to change its covers to match your outfit. There was no end. I mean, if you were not "put together" you were surely not "in." You had no excuse.

The positive side to this coordination compulsion was that at an early age I became aware of what went together and what didn't. You learned to do it on your own.

During my senior year of high school, I worked at Miller & Rhoads department store where I was a model and a salesperson, and often helped with the displays. I was bitten by the decorating bug once again. I walked around the store on my lunch hours and coffee breaks and made mental notes of displays in other departments. I often watched the display department in action. I saw them fuss and fidget until at last, with one final move, they stopped, obviously sensing that this was "it."

I remember my first trip to Paris. The young girls in their early teens impressed me so. They were simply dressed yet looked so chic —a short straight skirt, a simple jewel neck sweater, an oversized white shirt not tucked in, flat shoes, a pair of earrings, maybe a watch or simple bracelet, no makeup.

I remember my dad and his tattersall shirts, Harris tweed jackets, the special vest he always wore at Christmas, his insistence that no matter how much or how little you spent on something it should be of the best quality, and his famous exhortations (along with "Close the refrigerator door!") to "observe, observe, observe" and to "never lose your sense of humor."

Thinking about our pasts and writing down remembrances is therapeutic, and enlightening as well. In fact, in the process of recording remembrances, all sorts of feelings, visions, and hopes come to light. These can help in the process of making your house your true home, and a true reflection of yourself and your family.

The events of our lives form a pattern, a veritable blueprint that's yours to read as you see fit. Some of us are true to our pasts. Others try to conceal them. But the best houses seem to "come from the heart," and are created by people who know who they are and express it.

It has taken more than four hundred years to reach this apparent effortless state of perfection by a combination of luck and good management.

The Duchess of Devonshire, *The House: A Portrait of Chatsworth*

A papier-mâché hound adopted from a Nantucket shop is the master of this living room where furniture is covered in French fabric. Waxed terra-cotta tile floors contribute to the air of well-worn coziness. Homey touches abound. In the foreground, an English Victorian pillow softens the seat of a tufted English club chair, and a miniature wheelbarrow of potpourri sends off scent from atop the quirky black-and-white table by its side. The coffee table delights the eye of anyone who happens to sit down, decorated as it is with a pair of bronze doré candlesticks and a balustraded vase of roses. By the doorway, a carved wooden bird perches on a pile of books.

Taste is relative and is the sum total of the intellectual and emotional experiences of the individual. *Taste, in order to be positive and vital, must be exercised and developed. Taste is changeable and is influenced by environment. A highly cultivated taste, a taste that is knowledgeable and eclectic, is likely to be exciting and provocative, a personal taste at its highest level.*

Mrs. Eleanor Brown, *Finest Rooms*

I sit at this table in my dressing room and put myself together each morning. It is my place to relax and contemplate the day. Some of my favorite objects keep me company: a Queen Anne chinoiserie mirror, a small chinoiserie lacquer box, bottles of crystal and silver, the silver-backed mirror that I use every day, and a bronze doré mirror with a miniature painted on its ivory inset that's so old it's really just for admiring. My lamps were made from silver candlesticks decorated with the lion heads that are a recurring theme in my house and a testament to my love of the Regency period. The custom silk shades were made by Silver Dolphin in Houston. The Leipzig engravings of furniture and furniture decoration are framed with French mats and gold-leaf frames.

The kind of ambiance most people want today [is] an elegance gently tempered by nostalgia, by fantasy, by romance. The interesting things about these temperings is that they are wholly individualistic.
House and Garden, January 1968

29

II

INTERIORS SPEAK:
THE LANUAGE
OF THE
HOME

No house in America, inside or out, so completely

expresses the complicated, contradictory, even

inventive personality of its creator.

Mario Praz, describing Monticello,
the home of Thomas Jefferson,
in William Howard Adams's
Jefferson's Monticello

Coco Chanel spent a lifetime creating, in her own words, "poverty for millionaires, ruinous simplicity, the search for what does *not* attract the eye." She exploited knits, banned the corset, opted for simple sheaths over fussy clothes, bobbed her hair, and made suntans fashionable. She was a true renegade. Her declared mission was simple: simplify! She broke the rules and created new ones, and her spirit still endures.

Just as clothes should not upstage the person, objects should not upstage a room. The goal, then, of successful decoration should be the creation of a mood, an atmosphere, something far more intangible than the furniture we sit on and the objects we display. While we can describe objects and accessories in a room, we have far more trouble describing atmosphere. How many times have we found ourselves saying about a particular room, "It has something, but what? I can't quite put my finger on it."

Have you ever noticed how some rooms exude a certain energy, warmth, and a harmony of spirit? If you have, then you have experienced the language of the home. A language softly spoken, and universally understood.

Call it mood, atmosphere, feeling, or personality, whatever you wish, it is *this* quality, the balance between architecture and objects, that should define a space.

I suppose we have all had some sort of experience of communicating with a room. Sometimes we don't notice it immediately; it may be long after we've left that its effect suddenly takes hold. One

Photograph on previous page

Champagne, a magnificent view, and the luscious softness of this waterside window seat invite serious relaxation. The pillows are both old and new: antique Aubussons, Beauvais, and linen pillows mixed with plump new oversized chintz cushions. When the sun goes down, the beeswax candle in a French glass photophare sheds soft light on the antique table and chairs. The Chinese garden seat doubles as a side table or an extra chair.

Color, depth, and great warmth are the lures of this master bedroom. The fireside provides husband and wife a place to converse in peace and privacy. There's an ottoman for propping feet, small tables for coffee cups, and his-and-hers bookcases just an arm's length away. Standard brass reading lamps were "specialized" with ruby red fringe and fabric shades to match the room. The contrast of light walls and dark picture frames points up delicate Chinese silk paintings, while a bold mantel arrangement of greens and black provides a "punch line" in the room. Invitations are held by an antique English ornament made especially for that purpose. Green Wedgwood leaf plates are propped on cherub brackets. A dark pink hydrangea fills the fireplace in warm weather.

Why do we love certain houses, and why do they seem to love us? It is the warmth of our individual hearts reflected in our surroundings.

T. H. Robsjohn-Gibbings

COCO CHANEL

1883–1971

Cocteau wrote poems for her. Stravinsky played for her. Avedon and Beaton photographed her. She was Coco Chanel, who rose above her peasant past to become fashion's liberator.

In her early years a rich horseman, Étienne Balsan, helped the young Gabrielle Bonheur Chanel set up her business. Her hat shop just north of Paris quickly became popular with Balsan's rich friends.

It was the Roaring Twenties, when everything loosened up. Chanel felt that women had a right to be comfortable, and her trademark chemise was the beginning—shortened skirts, loose waists, and loads of costume jewelry. She took the sacred mourning color out from under wraps and created cocktail's "little black dress." The look she spawned remains ever popular and classic today.

Like her clothing, Chanel's quarters were opulent yet simple. Her apartment, above her fashion salon on the rue Cambon in Paris, is preserved just as it was when she was alive. The living room's Coromandel screens remain in place, and everywhere there are lions; her astrological sign; symbols of corn, which she considered good luck; her beloved deer; and religious artifacts.

Hibberd saw the "principles of taste" as "the subordination of every detail to the production of a complete effect, in which every contrast helps to conserve the harmony of the whole . . ."

Shirley Hibbard in *Rustic Adornments for Homes of Taste*

In a gentleman's study, the sculptural shapes of a basalt urn and a bronze of a horse stand out against decoratively painted walls and moldings. The sofa cushions trimmed with rope play host to antique needlepoint and silk taffeta pillows. Even the lampshade is tended to, edged with a simple gimp trim. The warm glow in this rich corner makes you want to curl up with a glass of port and a wonderful book.

remembers a certain serenity, an excitement, or perhaps, unfortunately, something that was disturbing or displeasing. We are aware of the subtleties of what makes a house a home. How we define *ourselves* is evidenced in our dress and in our homes. The way we look and the way we live are both the most potent and telling manifestations of who we really are.

By visiting museums that were once the homes of famous people, we are afforded the opportunity to glimpse how people once lived. We can study the architecture, the furnishings, and any objects or personal effects that remain. And when we leave we feel as if we have done more than just visit a museum, we feel as if we have experienced something.

On a recent antique-buying trip to England, France, and Sweden, I managed to secure some time for myself to see museums and famous houses. While all countries have their distinct history, heritage, and style, my trip to Sweden forced me to visually take note of the differences. I hate to be one to generalize, but if you were to categorize each country by its furniture, could you say that English is brown wood, French is gilt wood, and Swedish is painted wood?

The reason I mention this is by way of contrast. At Fontainebleau outside of Paris it is hard to grasp the vast scale and yet the intricacy of the work executed in the ballroom in the sixteenth century. The ballroom floor is precisely patterned like a mosaic, with a number of different woods, and the frescoed walls painted by Niccolò dell'Abbate depict mythological subjects. We view this and

The mood of a room must dictate. Every room has a mood or personality—sometimes latent—and it is this that one desires to develop.

Mrs. Eleanor Brown, quoted in *The Finest Rooms by America's Great Decorators*

In this house, the architecture leads the eye from one room to another: the vista from living room through the bedroom to a far dressing room wallpapered with a garden of sweet peas. The doorway itself commands attention. Its topside niche bears three Delft jars standing at attention. Seventeenth-century porcelains resting on wooden brackets mounted on the wall marry perfectly with the roughness of hand-hewn beams. Just visible in the dressing room is a Victorian shadow box bearing an intricate shell sculpture of a castle, and a quartet of Hogarth engravings.

A house, like a novel, is a small world defined against, but also reflecting, a larger one.

Philippa Tristam, *Living Space*

appreciate the fine artistry, but find it hard to relate to because the space is so very elaborate and grand.

My two favorite rooms at Fontainebleau are the Gallery of Diana, which was converted to a library by Napoleon III, and the Queen's boudoir.

The Gallery of Diana is a vast and glorious hall with painted, vaulted ceilings depicting scenes from French history. It is furnished with an enormous central table that beckons you to select a book and stay and read. *Rooms speak,* and this one spoke to me . . . any room full of books makes me want to linger, but this room, more than any other in the château, was real. I could feel the activity that had long since vanished.

The other room, considerably smaller, yet to me, the jewel of the château, was the Queen's boudoir. The silver background of the Pompeian-style painted panels glistened as they did in the peak of their glory. The curved ceiling was delicately painted. Each square in this mosaic framed a fragile flower, as if created for the finest piece of Sèvres.

A week later I walked through the royal palace in Stockholm and saw decorations and furnishings dating from the early eighteenth century. Grand in scale but simpler than those I saw in France, with more subdued colors and less gilt, but nevertheless incredibly beautiful. As I walked along reading my guide I happened on Oskar II's writing room, which supposedly has been kept exactly as the King left it when he died in 1907. It is a *very* Victorian room, and it is totally different from *anything* else in the palace. "High Victorian" is not my taste, but the leaflet describing this room had a loaded message—

> The interior design of the Writing Room is typical of the late 19th century desire for comfortable, homely surroundings. The multiplicity of small objects such as photographs of relatives and friends, ornaments, and everyday articles is part of the secret of the special atmosphere of the room.

Fontainebleau and structures of that ilk have left us with an enormous amount of data about their inhabitants, their wealth, whom they patronized. So many buildings of the same period have not remained intact. Wars, revolutions, neglect, theft, and abandonment have disbursed and destroyed their contents so we must read, research, and visit special exhibitions in order to put together a complete picture for ourselves. The beauty of King Oskar's writing room is that we can see *who* King Oskar was—what he liked, and with what he surrounded himself. We can do the same with every interior decorating magazine we pick up: We can see who people are, what they like, and how they live.

"Comfortable, homely surroundings . . ." says the leaflet, is what was typical of the end of the nineteenth century. The same can be said of today. Experts have long predicted this phenomenon and our expanding eclecticism in part proves this theory. We mix the past with the present, the handmade along with the high tech.

Up until the fifties, people bought furniture *en suite* from furniture stores. Today, one buys a table from one place, chairs from

Objects, yes. A perfect jungle of them . . . many books, too . . . But apart from a pair of andirons by Lipchitz and one minute oil by Dali, no signed objects, not one portrait, and not a single painting by a master.

Edmonde Charles-Roux, *Chanel* (New York: Knopf, 1975), p. 186.

another, and often waits for just the "right" sideboard to come along. The presence of treasured objects makes the difference between a room that is viewed as a "museum" and a room that is used for living.

The objects of a room—whether they are few or plentiful—are responsible for breathing life into a space. So in choosing objects for your rooms, steer clear of anything that's not really you.

I've seen my share of rooms that are overdone yet devoid of personality. If these rooms were people, I'd call them fashion victims. Here is a list of "decorating clichés" I find trite and overdone:

Don't be tempted to buy something just because it's the current style, because your decorator told you to, or because your decorator told you *not* to.

Instead, buy things that you like—things that speak to you. That way, you'll never go wrong.

In this bedroom, the frame of a chinoiserie mirror holds artful invitations, announcements, and thank-yous, turning them into part of the decor. Various objects in different shapes give this wall added interest and dimension. Wooden brackets hold two Delft jars; a trio of plates arches above; six architectural drawings depict views of London and important buildings there. The reading chairs plumped with antique cotton paisley pillows and a Kashmiri shawl invite curling up by the fire. The tole table on an iron stand contains all kinds of touchable treasures: a miniature rosewood commode inlaid with brass, ornate gilt metal candlesticks, and a pair of horn cups delicately engraved.

The desire for symmetry, for balance, for rhythm is one of the most inveterate of human instincts.

Edith Wharton and Ogden Codman, Jr., *Decoration of Houses*

Jim Steinmeyer 1983

THOMAS JEFFERSON

1743–1826

I am as happy nowhere else, and in no other society, and all my wishes end, where I hope my days will, at Monticello. Too many scenes of happiness mingle themselves with all the recollections of my native woods and fields to suffer them to be supplanted in my affections by any other.

Thomas Jefferson

Thomas Jefferson was truly a Renaissance man. Worldly and urbane, but at heart, a country gentleman who was most happy when rooting about his beloved gardens or concocting some new invention at Monticello in the Virginia hills.

Monticello was designed almost entirely by Jefferson. He based his original plan on classic sixteenth-century Italian houses. Later additions were inspired by the small, elegant houses he had seen in Paris. The house was chock-full of wonderful things, including French and English furniture, paintings, clocks, prehistoric mammoth bones, tools, and trees—all the accoutrements of a man of such diverse interests.

His crisp and practical tearoom was known as the "most honorable suite" because Jefferson used it as a trophy room of sorts. Here, he displayed busts of some of his favorite heroes. Benjamin Franklin, John Paul Jones, Lafayette, and George Washington. In the late afternoon, Jefferson could often be found reading and writing in the tearoom, at a revolving-top table of his own design.

A Venetian mirror on mirrored walls, a tiger-patterned velvet chair, and the marble-topped table and marble floor give this dressing room a dramatic flair. The friendly notes of clutter include a collection of silver perfume bottles, brushes, and boxes, some family photos, and a perpetual calendar that keeps track of busy days.

Photograph on opposite page

A mudroom with panache: besides the usual Wellington boots, hats, canes, and umbrellas, this mudroom offers a convenient desk lit by papier-mâché candlestick lamps from Kashmir, and bisque fish vases. Delft porcelain and a chalet calendar from 1888 decorate the wall.

EVERY PICTURE TELLS A STORY

The personality of a room hinges on its objects and accessories. Lamps, pictures, porcelains, and family heirlooms speak volumes about their owners.

Just for fun, play "Who Lives Here" for a moment: take a look at these three very different rooms, owned by different people. You'll discover a lot about the owners at a glance.

Notice the overall shell of the room—wall color, fabrics, carpet —as well as the small telling details, even the fireplace mantels. In fact, this architectural element was the basis for developing the three rooms. I think you'll agree with the old adage that every picture tells a story.

Red walls and lots of black and white accents are the background for the library of a theatrical set designer. Architectural bookcases, an antique oriental rug, oil portraits, and a formal chandelier set a tight and structured masculine tone. Busts of characters from plays perch around the room, keeping watch on the proceedings.

A stripped pine mantel and tattersall chairs set a casual tone in this family sitting room in the country. This is a gathering place, with a deep comfortable sofa, and plenty of chairs ready to pull up to the fire. On the fender, the children can warm themselves with a cup of hot chocolate after playing in the snow. A pile of photograph albums top the low pine coffee table. The window treatment is casual but elegant—a fringed swag hung from a simple wooden pole. A stately painting hangs over the fire. The needlepoint rug feels cozy underfoot.

Blue striped walls and the punch of a mahogany regency bookcase are among the outstanding aspects of this city living room—home to a mature, settled couple who love old books, old things, and each other. The room bears witness to a lifetime of thoughtful accumulating. Treasured blue-and-white porcelains are proudly displayed. The symmetrical surroundings speak to the owners' underlying orderliness. This is a retreat at the end of each day—a place to read the paper and have a drink before dinner. The basket of logs, plump upholstery, and the throw draped over the back of the chair invite return visits.

I hope this little exercise has given you a taste of a room's many layers, and how they speak louder than words.

Now look at your own house with new eyes. Is it saying what you want it to? Does it express you? Are you proud to open the door? Sometimes all your house needs is a little *exercise!*

Maybe the carpeting from a previous owner has always bothered you. Why not get rid of it, and enjoy bare floors and the hunt for a pleasing replacement? Perhaps some colorful pillows or a soft mohair throw would make your sofa more inviting. Doesn't your busy bathroom deserve better than peeling wallpaper? Sometimes the simple addition of a fresh beeswax candle or a fragrant bunch of eucalyptus can boost a tired room.

When you think of your house as an active machine, pulsing with the comings and goings of everyone who lives there or visits, it makes sense to give it regular tune-ups. The sight of your improvements will be a daily delight.

Photograph on opposite page

Encouraging self-expression at an early age is wonderful. In this bedroom, a young girl was urged to include her interests and accomplishments, favorite colors, and mementos to help create a room that is undeniably hers! It's plain to see that horses are a special love, and that hobby is reflected everywhere. For the fireplace, artist Anne Harris did the decorative painting of a horse and her foal. The fire screen is a decoupage of butterflies fluttering across pages cut from a book of old French nursery rhymes. And what little girl could resist sharing secrets on the Victorian confidante, newly recovered in a rose velvet with rope trim. Its pillow was made from a small piece of needlepoint, and the small side table was fashioned from a papier-mâché tray.

On top of an imposing Regency cabinet are a pair of ormolu and bronze urns and a bust, formally arranged and an orchid in a basalt cachepot. A water-gilded oval mirror hangs above, reflecting the stately scene.

WINSTON CHURCHILL

1874–1965

I am content for the first time in my life to look after my own affairs,
build my house, and cultivate my garden.

Winston Churchill

The scion of a beautiful American mother, the socialite Jennie Jerome, and a British father, Lord Randolph Churchill, Winston Leonard Churchill made a name for himself at a young age by escaping from a prisoner of war camp during the Boer War. Soon after, young Winston became a member of Parliament, and eventually the Prime Minister of England.

His home and haven was Chartwell, a red brick retreat on eighty acres in the countryside of Kent, just twenty-five miles from London. Here, Churchill could show the softer side of his nature, tending to his fruit trees, building a playground for his daughters, a swimming pool and a retirement cottage for himself and his wife, Clementine.

Sir Winston was a traditionalist. At first glance, his classic English drawing room at Chartwell might seem an odd setting for the blustery, outspoken Churchill. But its silken sofas and fine appointments were appropriate for the home of a mighty world leader, and helped contribute to the soothing, domestic atmosphere at Chartwell.

And when things were not all right with the world—which was often during Churchill's time—Chartwell stood as a true sanctuary for this complex extraordinary man.

What's so delightful about this guest cottage bedroom is its symmetry: the pillows, the lamps, the starburst mirror, prints of birds, and a pair of Wedgwood creamware plates, all arranged to delight the eye. The hand-painted bedside tables were specially made to fit the space. Their long, narrow shape makes them easy to reach.

If the 18th century is often described by architectural historians as the great age of the English house, the Victorian period might equally well be called the great age of the English home. Neither good taste nor wealth . . . can transform a house into a home, for a home does not consist in the quality of its architecture or decor, but in the quality of the lives that it expresses.

Philippa Tristam, *Living Space*

In a corner of Laura and John Pomerantz's sitting room, an English mahogany library table supports a magnificent volume, and the ivory-handled magnifying glass affords a closer look. The deep-buttoned ottoman covered in Fortuny fabric gets an extra measure of detail, edged with delicate rope and bullion fringe.

Photograph on opposite page

Two cobalt urns flank the antique Venetian mirror in this elegant bedroom. I think this is one of the few times I have honestly felt that "less is more." Once the urns and a centering bouquet of old-fashioned flowers were in place, the client's eye said, "It's right," and I have to admit, I agreed.

If a room can symbolize what a decorator is all about, this one speaks volumes about David Easton. Ever sensitive to the dynamics between architecture, decoration, and the landscape—design precepts firmly rooted in the eighteenth century—Easton always keeps these French doors open to the garden, weather permitting, and the flat of spring flowers blooming on the table is practically *de rigueur*.

A pair of painted chairs with checked cushions, a table, and a brass Gothic column lamp set the scene for relaxation and reading. Gimp-trimmed curtains frame the view. On display: a Wedgwood creamware plate and an early Minton fern plate.

. . . A house is but the normal expression of one's intellectual concept of fitness and his aesthetic ideal of what is beautiful.

Frank A. Parsons, *Interior Decoration: Its Principles and Practice*

III

UNDECORATING:
THE ATTENTION
TO DETAIL

It is perhaps not uninstructive to note that we have no

English word to describe the class of household ornaments

which French speech has provided with at least three

designations, each indicating a delicate and almost

imperceptible gradation of quality. In place of bric-a-brac,

bibelots, objets d'art, we have only knickknacks—

defined by Stormoth as "articles of small value."

Edith Wharton and Ogden Codman, Jr.,
The Decoration of Houses

OBJECTS GIVE A HOUSE CHARAC-
ter. We accumulate things over time.
We cherish them and display them prominently.
They are assimilated into our daily routine. A
paperweight. A brass change box. A bud vase.

This process, which some call decoration, is
really what I call "living." It is a progression, not
a single event.

I am always amused when people ask me,
"Is your apartment finished yet?" We moved

from a townhouse to a co-op apartment several years ago and had to do quite a bit of work. Well, the construction has long since been completed, but the living goes on.

I do not want to understate the importance of the decoration process by any means. Curtains, carpet, painting, and furniture all take time, effort, and money. They provide the foundation, the bones of a house, and whether you do it yourself or work with a professional, it makes no difference: The important thing to remember is that *your* house is *your* home. It must have your stamp —a charisma all its own—that *you* are responsible for creating. The extra step we take—sometimes at no extra cost or perhaps only a minute of time—can make the difference between the ordinary and the exceptional. Think about it: pens in a porcelain vase by the telephone, the perfume of a fragrant soap that lingers on the hands, a bowl of flowers in an empty corner—aren't these the civilizing touches that make everyday life a little sweeter?

Photograph on previous page

Richly constructed and colorful decorative trim can transform upholstery, drapery, pillows, loose chair seats, ottomans, table skirts, and lampshades in every room of the house.

Contrasting colors, picking up colors in the room in your trim, or keeping your palette monochromatic are all different and effective approaches.

In my guest bathroom, a tasseled tieback holds the floral shower curtain in place when it's not being used. The shower curtain is lined in a wavy blue-and-white stripe and trimmed with a periwinkle blue edging. The blue hydrangea topiary and a silver bowl filled with lavender softly perfume the air.

Take the time and do some small thing that will be noticed and remembered. Choose your objects carefully, and buy only what you *love*.

Until recently, furniture makers and fashion designers have always treated accessories as an afterthought, a sideline. But in truth, accessories are the most telling additions we give to our homes or our clothing.

The selection of fashion accessories enables us to distinguish our own personalities. A basic black cocktail dress can be transformed by the addition of a triple strand of pearls, fur cuffs, or a simple velvet belt with a rhinestone buckle.

In the same manner, decorative accessories can provide imagination and personality in a room with fine furniture and good architectural detail.

The economics of fashion and interior design have forced manufacturers to acknowledge that you can only buy a new sofa so many times. But the pillows that sit on it can be changed, added to, or moved to a different room for a different look, for little or no money at all.

Unfortunately, few of us even think about accessorizing our rooms until they are painted, filled with furniture, curtains, rugs, and the like. While waiting until the end isn't necessarily a bad idea, I've found that most people have run out of money, and sometimes steam, at this stage. The room is left without an inter-

OGDEN CODMAN, JR.

1863–1951

Born to a distinguished New England family, Ogden Codman, Jr., pursued his interests in architecture and decorating, and eventually snared some very prestigious clients, many of them through his social connections.

His work in Newport caught the eye of American author and society matron Edith Wharton, whose social connection gave her an inside look at the upper crust, and her sharp observations of their goings-on was the fodder for much of her writings.

Their collaboration, *The Decoration of Houses* (1897), is a treatise that made its mark by decrying Victorian stuffiness and espousing classicism.

The Codman family home, The Grange, in Lincoln, Massachusetts, was built as a Georgian mansion between 1735 and 1741. The house had been added on to over the years until it was more than double its original size. In 1862, Codman's father supervised Victorian-style alterations at The Grange. But during the 1890s, Ogden Codman, Jr., returned the house to its eighteenth-century appearance as much as possible. Symmetry, balance, and proportion were his watchwords. His sitting room at The Grange is an example of the Codman style at its best. The imported chintzes, columned fireplace, and fine oriental rug helped to create the refined atmosphere that was Codman's forte.

esting picture or a cachepot filled with flowers, and not a decorative cushion in sight, let alone some marvelous object.

Lack of time, money, and thought often cause us to make hasty and sometimes inappropriate selections. Take your time. Finishing a room by accessorizing it can either enhance the overall feeling or kill it. An empty tabletop or blank wall will recede, whereas one small picture on a large wall or some huge object on a delicate Sheraton table will glare at you from every point in the room.

So slow down. There is no race. Those who perceive a race may win it, but fail the test for "rooms that work."

If we view interior decoration as something we do throughout our lives—simply building the nest—then somehow the mystique should vanish. However, if we begin to worship our objects, their importance or their role in our lives becomes distorted. To credit one's significance to objects, and to allow those objects to upstage people is a cardinal sin.

FORGET THE RULES, AROUSE THE SENSES

Forget the decorating rules you have been carrying around with you. Instead, think about what you find pleasing. Think of the things you've found appealing in the rooms or houses you have visited. Evaluate how the senses can be stimulated to create a wonderful overall effect.

. . . A room should depend for its adornment on general harmony of parts, and on the artistic quality of such necessities as lamps, screens, bindings, and furniture.

Ogden Codman, Jr.

I love to see old textiles put to fine use, such as this fragment of a nineteenth-century silk Beauvais tapestry which was made into a glorious pillow.

All things green and gorgeous are gathered on this silk-draped table-top. The cut-out photographs of children always cause comment. Vegetable porcelains feel at home here—the plates shaped like lettuce and cabbage leaves, a cauliflower, a pair of pea pods, a painted clay turnip. The lamp was made from an alabaster architectural ornament. Casablanca lilies perfume the air.

Photograph below left

The details make this guest room a luxurious yet cozy nest. A lamp fashioned from an antique Chinese vase has a delicately smocked shade. The headboard cleverly combines taffeta and chintz with a multi-colored rope border. Sparkling on the bedside table are a few special silver objects, including a footed bowl filled with a gently fragranced potpourri. The walls are covered in chintz; the linens faintly detailed in pale yellow.

Photograph above right

A simple stepped arrangement can have great appeal when the objects are enticing and arouse all the senses. Here in my living room, lacquered chinoiserie nesting tables are topped by a saucer, a silver box, a framed Wedgwood plaque, and a silver urn filled with fragrant mimosa.

SIGHT. Things must be visually pleasing. Arrangement and color are key. And don't forget your sense of humor!

TOUCH. Vary the textures and finishes in your house. A cashmere throw that invites stroking or an intricately carved picture frame that arouses the curious eye are the sensory invitations a tactile house offers.

SMELL. Use scented candles, potpourri, and fresh flowers (the last, a double delight of sight and smell).

SOUND. Factor in a wind chime on an airy porch, a crystal bell on a tabletop. Even the sound of silverware as it is laid in a cloth-lined chest sounds a pleasing note. Decorating is like music. Harmony is what we constantly strive for. At home, we want a peaceful atmosphere where the objects are the notes and nothing is off-key.

Arrange objects to create visual excitement and stimulate the senses of touch and smell. Ask yourself these few questions: How do the objects relate to each other? How do they relate to the room? Where will they go, and how will they be viewed?

I don't like the term "tablescape"—it sounds too contrived—but there are a number of surfaces around the home that play host to arrangements of our "things." When it comes to creating these

Details *are the stuff that dreams are made of.*
Sarah M. Lockwood, *Decoration: Past, Present, and Future*

tablescapes, or, in gardening terms, "interior landscapes," there are no formulas, no right or wrong. You can put old with new, expensive with dimestore chic, rare and ordinary side by side in a relaxed way.

Arranging objects in a pleasing way may seem like sleight of hand if you're a little uncertain of your skill. But the basic goal behind the magic is this:

I. ACHIEVE BALANCE. Shapes are important. See what works well together. Round with rectangular? Narrow, high objects with long, low ones?

As for size, generally keep taller and heavier items in the rear. And experiment with groups of many small objects (the group of boxes in my home is one of my favorites) or a few large ones (sturdy andirons and a fan in front of a fireplace come to mind).

Look at colors. Sometimes one-color arrangements are striking, such as a group of celadon bowls. Adding a scarlet vase sounds a different note—one that can be just as pleasing.

Mixing textures is always interesting: A pile of old books on a marble-topped table, peaches in a wooden bowl.

Finally, don't overlook the power of juxtaposition. Balance opposites. An arrangement with spark combines old and new, rare and everyday, a flea market find and a family heirloom. Each item becomes more special with a contrasting partner at its side. It's kind of like arranging dinner guests at the table! Or like cooking. Occasionally you must stir the pot and perhaps add a dash of spice or add a garnish to the plate. In decoration, this means rearranging the furniture or the items on a tabletop to get a fresh look—and maybe adding a new item or something with wit.

II. AVOID MONOTONY. Break up matched or themed symmetrical sets with something unrelated; the odd piece is your visual exclamation point.

An example: the silver tea set placed, not on a silver tray, but on a sturdy, oval oak one.

On a larger scale, I remember a client who inherited a wonderful old bed with matching dresser. Although both pieces were attractive on their own, when paired they looked old-fashioned and staid. Bringing in a hand-painted chest of drawers for the bedroom, and stationing the old dresser in the downstairs foyer gave each piece a place to shine.

But beware. Free-form arrangements can often look contrived and self-conscious, and spin off into messiness. A table full of framed photographs, added to indiscriminately and generally ignored, can grow as weedy as an untended garden. Just as a picture is created by adding a dab of paint at a time, the best arrangements are created a step at a time, with pauses so you can step back and see the overall effect.

III. BE SPONTANEOUS, AND AD LIB. The best arrangements sometimes do just happen: the ottoman that doubles as a coffee table might be a cliché, but it works, or a miniature chest that can be used as a side table.

The successful *ad lib* in interior decoration is the result of an open mind. It's finding creative solutions to decorating problems or creating new uses for the things we have in the house. But objects are only as flexible as the people who possess them. If you are not flexible, the process stops there.

IV. OBSERVE. Develop your eye by studying books, magazines, catalogues, store displays, museums, and even the homes of your friends. Confidence, knowledge, and practice are the keys to successful arrangements. Decorating is like math, a game of adding and subtracting. But when you have successfully arranged a grouping, don't forget to reevaluate and move things around occasionally. As you "shuffle the deck" you increase your skills and confidence, and keep your rooms fresh and interesting. A clever arrangement achieves several goals. Most importantly, you are pleased with it. The objects look like they are relating and communicating. The arrangement continues to stimulate your imagination and the imagination of others. And it gives your room the wit that furniture alone cannot necessarily provide.

Like a garden, a house is organic and constantly evolving. For that reason, you must take to heart the principle of "undecorating." The late interior designer Billy Baldwin coined that word to emphasize a point: all the necessary elements of a room should not arrive on installation day. Room should always be left for the things we will acquire . . . the objects we cannot live without.

Decorating is like gardening. When you plant flowers, shrubs, or trees, it takes a while before they mature and create the borders and hedges you desire. Don't forget to weed and prune! In decoration, this means starting with a good foundation and being patient. Buy quality, and eventually you will have the look you want. If by chance you buy something that just doesn't work, get rid of it.

It may sound contradictory, but rooms can be beautiful without being "perfect." If a room is "done" to the last detail, the room looks stiff and studied, not to mention forbidding. If a room is left unfinished, somehow it will always exhibit youth.

The notion that there is the possibility for growth, that the room is alive, is promising and refreshing at the same time.

DUCHESS OF WINDSOR

1896–1986

She was a Baltimore divorcée. He was the King of England. After an eleven-month reign, he abdicated the throne to marry her. Thus, Wallis Warfield Simpson made her name.

The King's successor, his brother, refused to give Mrs. Simpson royal rank. But the Duke wanted his wife to use the royal title, and insisted to friends and employees that she be treated with due respect.

They retreated to a life in Paris, with a country house and a city mansion, the Duchess from the American South brought her own definite style to this new life. She played the part of a Duchess as if she were born to the role. Sheets freshly ironed each day, the finest food and drink, and a circle of friends hand-picked for their talents and social rank surrounded the Duke and Duchess of Windsor.

In her homes, the Duchess was always surrounded by flowers. White arum lilies, orchids, carnations, roses, ivy, and sunflowers were her favorites. In her ice-blue dressing room, the porcelain cachepots and silver vases always held fresh blooms. To further the effect, each of her rooms was scented with a perfume burner.

For a woman known as a fashion plate ("I only buy about a hundred new dresses a year," she once countered), her dressing room was her staging area, her preparation center. There, surrounded by mirrors and her paintings of lovely women of the past, the woman with the simple chignon prepared herself to confront a world that was always watching.

In my bedroom, the hand-painted bedside table is illuminated by a Paris porcelain lamp with a fringed silk shade. A nineteenth-century watercolor of a rose rests on an easel. The mix of pictures on the wall includes an oval floral watercolor, a German oil of a floral still life, and pencil sketches and ink drawings of nineteenth-century ladies, including French socialite Madame Récamier.

The flower arrangement of miniature Italian roses, scabiosa, sweet peas, and yarrow provides temptation to the rabbit on my brass match striker.

Sometimes a tabletop can say more than words about home and heritage. On this inlaid table in the living room, family photographs in
antique silver and glass frames sound a nostalgic note. Wooden boxes are
shaped like books. The gardenia in full bloom exudes a heady fragrance.
The neoclassical figure on a recamier is made of translucent alabaster.

The old pine mantel in artist Clare Potter's living room hosts a variety of treasures. The miniature wooden hand-carved chairs look so merry you almost expect them to start dancing. Small watercolors of roses, a tray painted with morning glories, and a tole silhouette of a vase and flowers make a little indoor garden. Over the mantel, a nineteenth-century English painting, *A Fishing Party,* is bordered by pink-trimmed English plates on the left, and reticulated creamware plates on the right. An antique doll keeps a vigilant eye on this delicate collection.

Decor must have sentimental value. A house must tell a story.

Mark Hampton, *Harper's Bazaar,* June 1989

The best kitchens are filled with a mix of functional and decorative objects. The idea is to display what you have, and use it, too.

An Edwardian what-not in the niche of this kitchen decoratively displays a variety of kitchenware, including flower containers, plates, tureens, and a cookbook library.

On the top shelf, white ceramic Victorian posy holders shaped like branches and logs keep company with a pair of tooled brass cachepots, English porcelain botanical plates, a big basket of brushes and scrub straws, and painted metal lamps with gilded decoration. In the midst of it all, a rooster perches on a lidded dish.

The walls have not been neglected either. There is a Victorian needlepoint of hunters with their dogs, and two majolica leaf plates on either side of a hand-carved bracket. The pair of leather frames are so wonderful on their own that pictures would be superfluous.

The German tole cutouts on the side walls are thought to have been funereal in nature.

Photograph on opposite page

Balderbrae is decorator David Easton's Hudson Valley home. In the Great Hall, the wall between two French doors displays a marvelous collection of objects from around the world. The triple candle sconce of a lion's head and snakes is a copy of a Regency design in the collection of the Victoria and Albert Museum. A collection of nineteenth-century English transferware, creamware, and Delft plates and dishes is a disparate group that looks wonderful together. Below them is a pair of eighteenth-century engravings of French philosophers; their dark frames contrast with the creamy walls. On the half-round table, a small column lamp with a silk shade sheds light on a creamware plate, a twentieth-century French porcelain cabbage, and two stacks of books.

Sometimes placement is everything. These Staffordshire King Charles spaniels stand at attention atop columns, drawing the eye upward and calling attention to the architecture of the cabinets. At the same time, juxtaposing colors—light dogs against dark walls—makes the figures more striking.

The balanced arrangement in this bathroom shows how satisfying a well-thought-out composition can be. Each carefully chosen object seems to have its own story to tell.

The sink was dropped into an old washstand. Two brown ceramic vases hold roses that are replenished almost daily. The antique oval mirror is surrounded by blackamoor sconces, majolica plates, and watercolors, and another framed watercolor of tulips is propped on the basin behind a votive-filled ceramic basket.

Viewed from above, this brass galleried coffee table looks as pleasing as a framed still life. The true-life elements: a pair of bronze dog candlesticks, creamware leaf plates, a Victorian match striker, and a silver-and-bone-handled magnifying glass on top of an irresistible book. The ceramic basket cachepot, tightly packed with roses and ivy, looks just like a garden gate.

A huge bouquet of dried hydrangeas explodes like Mount Vesuvius in the center of the living room, nested in the middle of a velvet-draped round table. The table is a place to show off favorite books and wonderful things to look at, such as turtle shells, a model rowboat, a miniature wheelbarrow, and a porcelain basket of trompe l'oeil bread and butter. Each stack of books acts as a pedestal, giving the objects museum-like importance.

Photograph below

For the nineteenth-century giltwood table in my foyer, I made a lamp from a carved and gilded architectural ornament—one of a pair I found in England. The top of the ornament became the lamp's finial. I wanted a shade that wouldn't detract from the base of the lamp, and I think this simple oval one was the answer. The mural was painted by artist Anne Harris; I call it my low-maintenance city garden. Every day when I leave and return home I pass through my garden—an oasis filled with clematis, lily of the valley, and foxgloves, and only steps from the bustle of New York City streets.

Good dressing is largely a question of detail and accessories.
Elsie de Wolfe

Photograph on opposite page

In a young lady's bedroom, a special corner with a window is devoted to "making up." A kidney-shaped dressing table skirted in chintz epitomizes feminity. The windows, chair, and lampshade all wear the same attire—Floral Bouquet by Lee Jofa. The hanging shelf displays porcelains, and miniature houses from Bermuda. When the silver trumpet vases hold roses, the magic is complete.

I n this guest bedroom, six delicate stipple engravings of lilies by Redouté, with giltwood frames and French mats, make a strong statement when grouped together. In fact, the way they are placed, they are almost an extension of the headboard.

Some objects take on more importance when grouped together. Here, treasures of oriental origin have found their way to a Venetian side table painted with neoclassical figures. There's a celadon vase, a miniature ivory barrel, a bottle painted on the inside with Chinese figures, and another small lidded celadon dish. The lamp has a distressed finish that contrasts with the delicacy of all the other items. A shagreen cabinet adds richness in the background.

I may create a very disciplined background, but then I like things messed up or cozied up a little. I am always thinking of warmth.

David Hicks

Lions—this time on a coat of arms that decorates this rather commanding needlepoint pillow. The French tole tray table is just the right size for a cup of coffee, and its painted design offers something to look at when the table is not being used. For a little extra emphasis, I outlined the sofa cushions with multi-colored rope trim; it's the decorative equivalent of a highlighting pen!

The corner of this bookcase holds two watercolors. The French cavalry officer, by nineteenth-century artist Clement Auguste Andrieux and an English eighteenth-century watercolor of two gentlemen in conversation. The Regency-style candlestick lamp with red silk shade casts a warm glow.

I like to give my guests good reading light, a stack of books—old favorites as well as recent acquisitions—and some pretty things to look at. Here, it's a plate of seashells collected on family trips, a red papier-mâché dish, and a soothing engraving of a woman napping on a park bench. The rose topiary reflects the rose chintz of the upholstered headboard and table skirt. On the bed is an antique Marseille cloth, dyed deep blue for the room. A Wedgwood candlestick converted to a lamp provides a note of punch against a pale pink wall.

The special detail on this floral shower curtain is its contrasting scal-loped edge. A lacy Victorian wire planter keeps embroidered towels close at hand.

Photograph on opposite page

For a garden-like feeling, this bath is detailed with lots of floral touches. Sconces were painted in the colors of the room, and their shades match the rose-patterned fabric at the windows. Accenting the towels are light pink and blue bows, and the theme in enhanced by the painted mirror, with its hand-carved garlanded hanger. Latticed radiator covers add to the garden-like mood.

The wallpaper is an aqua-colored interpretation of faux bois whose subtle patterns also resemble rippled water.

Everyone carries his own inch-rule of taste and amuses himself by applying it, triumphantly, wherever he travels.

Henry Brooke Adams, *The Education of Henry Adams*

95

In this Long Island house, a tropical mural by Graham Rust is a creative combination of real and faux. It looks as though this mirrored-back sconce in the shape of the sun is suspended by a ribbon. But the ribbon, leaping monkey, tented walls, and tall cooling palms swaying in the breeze are actually painted on the wall.

In this bedroom, a chaise upholstered in a richly embroidered silk is the seat of honor. A tole and brass lamp encrusted with porcelain flowers is topped with a shade of soft stippled green. Billowy white balloon shades, bordered by iridescent taffeta curtains let in the light by day and create a moody atmosphere when drawn in the evening. The antique basket on the painted satinwood table is made of carved ivory.

Sometimes the simplest details can have maximum effect. For the bench at the end of a bed, the cushion edges have been carefully outlined with rope, the corners dramatically finished with a spiraled knot and tassels.

IV

ESSENTIAL ELEMENTS:
COMFORT
PASSION
AND
HUMOR

What is needed is a sense of domesticity . . .

a feeling of privacy . . .

an atmosphere of coziness . . .

Witold Rybczynski, *Home*

IN MY WORK AS A DECORATOR, I HAVE come to the conclusion that the best rooms contain three essential ingredients: this is my Room Recipe.

Just as I never set to cooking without my notes, utensils, and all the ingredients by my side, I never leave a room I'm working on until it contains *comfort, passion,* and *humor.*

With these, a room will sizzle and smile. Without them, you may have a good-looking

Ah! There is nothing like staying home for real comfort.

Jane Austen, *Emma*

room, but a room that, somehow, never really works. The sofa should say, Come sit. The objects should say, Take a closer look, I'm really something special. The books, Look through my pages. The ottoman, It's okay to prop your feet here. In other words, Enter, make yourself at home.

At home. Isn't that the key? Many people forget that their house is their home—their own nest.

I'm sure you've heard stories about people who have not moved a thing since the decorator placed it there on installation day. The point is, these people lack the confidence to move something *in their own house!* Can you imagine how agonizing it must have been for both client and decorator when they went out together to shop for special things for the house?

How can a room assembled and maintained in this manner ever express the personality of its owner?

Photograph on previous page

One of my favorite corners of the house is in my bedroom. Curled up on my chaise with my books and a pot of tea, wrapped in the cashmere cable throw with my dogs napping nearby, I am truly content. The three-tier mahogany table holds lots of books and family photographs. On the top shelf you'll see a nosegay of primroses tied with an old ribbon. I've put this very special gift in a very special place where I can see it from every corner of my room. The lamp is made from an oriental vase. The pillows on my chaise are a comfortable union of antique needlepoint and new chintz.

Everyone says comfort is their goal when decorating, but many fail. Here are some of the culprits:

The eighteenth-century chairs with delicate spindly legs originally intended for the ballroom and brief stays between dances do not exactly beckon as you look for a place to sit and linger.

Objects so strategically arranged that you dare not pick one up for closer inspection because you may forget its "proper" place.

The lamps you could never read by because their wattage is geared toward setting some sort of mood first.

The sofa or chair with so many pillows that you teeter on the edge.

And finally, there is the room that asks, Does anyone live here? In other words, there are no signs of the owner in sight. Some of these rooms look like hotel lobbies or the wing of some museum. You sense the imaginary ropes and stanchions telling you where you are permitted to tread.

In all these examples, there is a vacuum, a void, a certain something missing. That something is not a thing—it is the welcome that should await you at the threshold.

Now that you're aware of what comfort *isn't,* let me tell you what I think comfort means. You may agree with me on some points, differ with me on others, and will probably add some ideas of your own. The important thing is to factor *comfort* into all your decorating plans.

COMFORT IS . . .

Soft inviting chairs for sitting.

Adequate lighting. I know this sounds boring, but let's face it—if you don't have proper light you can't see anything that might otherwise be enjoyed.

Personal possessions: mementos of a family vacation, a treasured bargain from a country auction.

A beckoning pile of pillows that invites you to nap or just lean up against them and relax.

Plants and flowers that re-create the out-of-doors and warm sunny days, no matter what the weather.

A desk with all the tools you need to write letters, pay bills, write in your journal.

Warmth created through color—whatever colors put you at ease.

A convenient table to put a drink on.

A pot of tea, a good book, a comfortable chair near a sunny window.

When personality and perfection collide, personality should always win out. That's what I mean when I talk about decorating with passion. You love flowers? Show them. You've had dogs in your family since the day you were born? Use them as a theme in your decorating. Do you like to needlepoint? Then bring out those pieces and have them finished off. *That's* decorating with passion!

Passion is what you need to be good, an unforgiving passion.
David Easton

Objects should be an expression of enthusiasm. They are a clear declaration of your interests and the things that are dear to your heart. Some people display their teapot collections. Others like gameboards, tapestries, perfume bottles, or old books. Whatever your passions are, let them show. In decorating, it's all right to wear your heart on your sleeve. But objects are very powerful decorating tools. Their selection and arrangement can provide a room with its humor, wit, and passion.

Like people, the objects in a room should be mobile. Adding new ones to an arrangement brings vitality to the group.

Best of all, the objects will exude energy because of the creative way you've arranged them.

When we talk about decorating with a sense of humor, what we really mean is decorating with wit and a touch of whimsy.

This doesn't mean that something in your room should make you chuckle with laughter. But some object should cause you to do a double take. Perhaps a caricature, a sculpture, or the arrangement of a group of objects.

When I see something lighthearted in a room, I feel an immediate affinity for the person who put it there. These objects speak, without a word being spoken.

Now some people are more sober and serious. You may feel this kind of "humor" is not for you. But don't discount the theory. Other touches can be just as amusing, and can even make light of

Jim Steinmeyer 1990

ELSIE DE WOLFE, LADY MENDL

1865–1950

Almost single-handedly, Elsie de Wolfe changed the face of American decorating forever. She put style, luxury, and fashion into the house without sacrificing a bit of comfort.

Hundreds of high-society homes shook off Victorian excess in favor of a lighter look. Pale eighteenth-century French furnishings, white woodwork, and plain moldings were embraced because of an enterprising American actress who discovered her drama played just as well in the living room as it did on stage.

Her marriage late in life to the British Embassy's press attaché, Charles Mendl, gave her a title but her rich friends, who became her clients, gave her a name.

Lady Mendl was a close friend of the Duchess of Windsor, and was her "personal shopper" of sorts, guiding the Duchess in her clothing and decorating purchases. The Duchess obediently bowed to de Wolfe's impeccable taste—as did most of the world!

The venerable Colony Club on Madison Avenue was one of Elsie's first decorating assignments. She snared this plum simply by the force of her own bold style at home, which captured the attention of such influential sorts as architect Stanford White, whose firm just happened to be the Colony Club's designer.

Even small rooms fell under the Elsie de Wolfe spell. Her own bathroom in Paris was treated like any other room in the house. She stopped at nothing to create glamour and comfort in *every* room of the house.

your disposition—a kind of "I know it and you know it and let's laugh about it" approach.

My younger stepson gave me a miniature gold Rolls-Royce. He said it was a reminder for me to work hard and beat last year's sales record. It occupies a prominent place on my desk and surely makes people wonder.

The stone squirrel in my foyer makes people take another look, and the turtle shells on New York designer David Easton's center table have the same effect. Both of them quietly say, Everything does not have to be so serious.

When we feel it's okay to be ourselves, it is only natural that this process should begin at home—in our own homes.

Never underestimate the power of the pronoun *our* . . . nothing in your house will ever be interesting unless you have given it your personal stamp. Your own personality and sense of humor should be obvious. Add this to good books, fresh flowers, some candlelight, and you have instant warmth, comfort, and the confidence that comes from having done it yourself.

Photograph on opposite page

An azalea topiary strikes just the right note of softness and light in the corner of this sunny sitting room. Floor-to-ceiling chintz curtains have a thirties air. A carved Bavarian bear hat rack holds straw hats for everyone. The damask-patterned chintz chair, colored like sapphires, extends an invitation to sit.

. . . the test of a home is whether it makes the visitor feel at ease.

Philippa Tristam, *Living Space*

This quiet corner is reserved for a welcome guest, with all the things I'd like for myself if I were visiting: a cozy chair, a magazine, a cup of tea, fresh flowers. After all, one of the nicest ways of saying welcome is to interpret our own style for our guests. Like a quietly well-dressed woman wearing a pair of spunky socks, this cozy chair and ottoman get their dash from a rope trim of many colors. A piece of antique Aubusson is finished with velvet to create a sumptuous pillow and an elegant support.

Comfort is perhaps the ultimate luxury.
Billy Baldwin

The fanciful red table next to this chintz-covered slipper chair is a reader's delight, just begging to hold a pile of books-in-progress. On the wall, an arrangement of eighteenth-century Swedish bird prints hangs with a pair of painted leaf plates. Two sculptures of horn on brass mounts look like trumpet flowers in full bloom on the table. The print propped behind the English candlestick lamp is a colored graph done for embroidery for the *Englishwoman's Domestic Magazine*.

A pleated fabric lampshade gives a standard brass floor lamp special treatment in one corner of my guest room. On the scalloped painted table sits an engraving of Paris on an easel and a collection of porcelain and enamel boxes. For the club chair I chose a stripe from Manuel Canovas. The pillow made from a bouclé fabric was a gift. The small slogan needlepoint pillow tells the world of my affection for dogs. Morning glories are depicted in the eighteenth-century engraving by John Edwards, and greet my guests each morning just as if they were in the country.

Photograph on opposite page

Pillows on a bed are nothing new, but an eclectic mix of pillows in different shapes, colors, and textiles create an interesting nest. Used in abundance, pillows give a lush, comfortable look.

On the hand-carved four-poster bed in my own bedroom, an antique Aubusson of tulips sits center stage, in front of a large European square covered in antique lace; each panel depicts a different animal. I added the pink quilted cotton covers for a dash of deep color and tucked the white lace pillows behind. The collection is completed by my Porthault lily of the valley neckroll and heart-studded boudoir pillow.

MARK TWAIN

1835–1910

Samuel Clemens, America's Mark Twain, found refuge in his family and in his home.

In 1874, he, his wife Olivia and three daughters moved into a house in Hartford, Connecticut, built especially for them by an eminent architect of the day, Edward T. Potter.

The huge red brick Victorian home was larger and more decorative than most residences at that time, but it was as suitably dramatic as the sealskin coat and hat the ebullient Clemens was fond of wearing.

The master bedroom in the Clemens house was a place of retreat for the adults. An intricately carved double bed bought in Venice was the centerpiece of the room. It is said that Twain and his wife used to lie with their heads at the foot of the bed so they could admire their fancy headboard decorated with cherubs.

Twain was often photographed reading and writing in bed, an activity which in those days was considered a bit eccentric. From beneath the bedclothes, he dictated his autobiography. Many of Twain's most popular books were written at this house: *The Adventures of Tom Sawyer, The Adventures of Huckleberry Finn, The Prince and the Pauper, Life on the Mississippi,* and *A Connecticut Yankee in King Arthur's Court.*

Samuel Clemens died in his magnificent bed on April 21, 1910, the day after Halley's comet appeared in the sky.

Books are beautiful things.
George Bernard Shaw

This family loves books and art, so lots of corners in their house are devoted to comfortable reading. This particular corner features a plump French chair and ottoman, both covered in Fortuny fabric; the needlepoint cushion provides punch as well as support. A black chinoiserie floor lamp casts the right amount of soft light. The side table was made from an eighteenth-century box delicately painted with grisaille landscape. Venice is a particular passion of the family, as evidenced by the 1855 James Holland painting *The Piazetta*, which keeps company with leatherbound volumes in the bookcase.

I'll always put in one controversial item, it makes people talk.

Dorothy Draper

The framed needlepoint above this bed, and the piles of books in the room, suggests that the room's occupant and the Victorian gentleman pictured are kindred spirits. Dogs are a passion, too, as evidenced by the embroidered spaniel on the wall and the plaster statue sporting his own bow-tied ribbon collar on the bedside table. Antique pillow shams set off the unusual bed, which juxtaposes an upholstered headboard with tall, bare iron posts. The pair of bell pulls reminds us of the days when breakfast was summoned by a gentle tug.

115

A desk takes on a special look when its accessories are thoughtfully chosen, and used in unexpected ways. Here, a Chinese vase converted to a lamp is topped by a dark green silk shade. The silver toast rack holds letters. A delicate spill vase is put to good use holding pens and pencils. Though the antique inkwells aren't used anymore, they are lovely to focus on during pensive moments, and for securing a stack of papers. Items collected at different times, in different places, come together in one place to create a space that works in more ways than one.

Photograph on opposite page

Displaying like things together can make for an interesting grouping. On the left, from top to bottom, is a Victorian papier-mâché box inlaid with mother-of-pearl, a rosewood Regency bank given to my husband as a gift, and a painted box found at a tag sale for $1.50! In the center is a satinwood painted box found at auction and a box made of various woods. On the right, from top to bottom, is a chinoiserie lacquered tea caddy, a lacquered box, and a small painted box I bought because it has campanula flowers on the lid.

On a trip to England, my husband and I bought this Regency secretary for our living room. When I sit in the living room to read I often use the secretary to jot down notes or write a postcard or two. Most of the gardening books were inherited from my grandmother. Most of the leaf plates are late eighteenth-century Coalport, while the one on the far right is from a contemporary artist. I'm intrigued by vegetable and fruit porcelains. I think it's the touch of whimsy interpreted in such a strong and durable medium. I call these porcelains my twentieth-century Chelsea—the antiques of the future. The porcelains and clay sculptures were made by Lady Anne Gordon, Mary Kirk Kelly, and Katherine Houston. Near the lamp, more treasures from England: a spill vase of flowers and a small framed Wedgwood plaque. I pick up postcards at museums everywhere and put them in the desk. I use them for notes, gift cards, and bookmarks, and my house guests like reviewing the stack and carefully selecting their own to write a few notes themselves.

On English style: "It can reconcile the good with the bad, the rare with the commonplace, the handsome with the homely more successfully than any other national style."
John Richardson

BILLY BALDWIN

1903–83

S mall in stature, with a giant-size talent, Billy Baldwin was the dean of American decorating. He was cocky and self-confident, and admitted he considered himself superior to most.

He started working for his family's decorator in Baltimore, but his talent was soon recognized in New York. In no time, he had signed on as apprentice to the indomitable Ruby Ross Wood, one of the premier decorators of the day. And from there, his fortune unfolded.

When you ignore the logic of the eye, the result may be a room that is disastrously uncomfortable even though it is undeniably beautiful.

With pronouncements such as this, and a talent to match, Billy Baldwin secured his position as one of America's most innovative and influential interior designers, who set new standards for the rooms we live in. His trademark slipper chair is still considered a decorating classic, and is a testament to the timelessness of his eye.

His own library in New York was an example of Baldwin at his best. The room had a whole wall full of books, which he considered a far better accent than any wallpaper could ever hope to be! And as always, there was a touch of the exotic—the gilded screen, the animal-skin rug—for dash and fun. The linen-and-toast colors (He had a heart of beige, said one admirer), rattan tray tables, and practical swing-arm lamp were all Billy basics. The result: simple, stylish comfort. Irresistible.

Photographs below

Because I love flowers, I find myself gathering things that carry out that theme. On this tabletop, (below right) it's roses, roses everywhere. The centerpiece is a platter ringed with roses, with an armorial center. Full-blown roses dried in silica gel nest in front, near a rose-footed teacup and a silk rose and butterfly based in a ceramic vase made of leaves. The pitcher and plate are nineteenth-century English porcelains. The small rose watercolor is Victorian. And because I love real flowers as much as I do, I can't resist buying things to put them in. As you can see, I seem to gravitate toward things that are urn-shaped, whether it's Georgian silver or a campana-shaped English porcelain.

Photograph on opposite page

A garden can grow anywhere, even far from real soil. Here in my own home, auriculas, primulas, polyanthus, and primroses set a tabletop ablaze with color. Artist Clare Potter made the clay auricula, which was given to me as a gift. The porcelain spill vase probably pleased a nineteenth-century woman as much as it pleases me. A turn-of-the-century English painting, an eighteenth-century English School pencil drawing, and an engraving propped against the wall provide a flowering backdrop.

Hollyhocks in all mediums—whether painted, engraved, or sculpted from clay—remind me of one of my favorite cottage garden flowers. I'm especially sentimental about the M. E. Young painting of hollyhocks in a walled garden. I bought the painting at auction in England; it was the first painting purchased for our house in the country. The English silver watering can and shovel on top of my gardening books are the beginning of what will no doubt end up being a collection of tiny gardening tools. The fabric, which includes hollyhocks, is another of my nineteenth-century chintzes, which happens to be part of a set of curtains.

At my house, fruits and vegetables come in all shapes and sizes. They are delicate, colorful, whimsical, and tempting. The stipple engravings of apples usually hang in my kitchen. I bought the blue-and-white platter in England for my country house. The porcelain saucer and plate are among my English finds. The eighteenth-century French faience melon tureen coexists quite happily with newer varieties, such as the porcelain lemon, peach, and melon by Lady Anne Gordon and the clay grape cluster, apple, and kumquat by Mary Kirk Kelly.

A group of equestrian prints are skillfully hung in a simple stair-step pattern.

Framed between two doors in a bedroom, this painted antique chest looks as though it was made to fit the space in theme and size. Proclaiming the owner's personal passions are a wallpaper-covered box personalized with her name, a plate decorated with horses, and one important Victorian watercolor on the wall.

In the bedroom of a feminine young lady, the fireplace wall displays current equestrian interests and childhood pastimes. Artist Anne Harris painted the fireplace with a portrait of the young lady's horse. Above, a specially made stuffed bear and fabric-covered picture frames keep company with Beatrix Potter figurines, a John Goodall watercolor, and polka-dot shaded sconces specially made to match the room.

Like a beautiful rose garden viewed from the air, this gracefully shaped papier-mâché tray table hosts flowers of every sort. A group of papier-mâché hand-decorated boxes rests near a pair of English porcelain plates. The amethyst bottle is filled with roses picked from the garden that morning.

Each item in a collection has its own story, its own memory—the search, the day you bought it, who you were with, the vacation, etc.; a collection provides a special satisfaction and sense of achievement.

Tricia Guild and Elizabeth Wilhide, *Tricia Guild's Design and Detail*

The flower that inspired a thousand more: artist Clare Potter found this early nineteenth-century porcelain dinner service, probably Spode, in a New York City shop. The charm and realism are what inspired her to try her hand at re-creating a lifelike clay version. Today, such clay sculptures are her specialty, and these provocative pansies have an honored spot center stage amid the porcelains.

Because her husband, Nick, complained that he had to go to other people's houses to see her work, artist Clare Potter burned the midnight oil in secrecy, sculpting and painting an assortment of her signature fruits and flowers as a Christmas gift for him. Today, they are the centerpiece of the Potters' dining room table, gently nestled in sterling silver baskets.

Nothing *is interesting unless it is personal. If you really like something, you can usually find a place for it—but maybe not the one you had in mind.*

Billy Baldwin

DIANA VREELAND

1903–1989

Red. It was the favorite color of fashion's high priestess with the extraordinary mouth, Diana Dalziel Vreeland.

Whether she was serving as editor in chief of *Vogue* or directing the Metropolitan Museum of Art's Costume Institute, as she did in later years, Mrs. Vreeland could always be counted on for her unerring eye, her flair for the unusual, and an unforgettable phrase that summed it all up.

"Pink is the navy blue of India," she proclaimed, and queried, "Why don't you wash your child's hair in last night's champagne?" Confident statements such as these made her famous for much longer than her friend Andy Warhol's proverbial fifteen minutes.

When she decorated the living room of her Park Avenue apartment, Mrs. Vreeland gave her decorator, Billy Baldwin, an explicit charge. "I want . . . a garden," she said. ". . . a garden in hell." His answer: a red Persian chintz from Colefax and Fowler that covered almost everything in the room. Incense filled the air. Her favorite needlepoint pillows were stacked in tiers on the sofa.

In the introduction to *Vogue's Book of Houses, Gardens, People*, Vreeland wrote: "Few things are more fascinating than the opportunity to see how other people live . . ." In describing the people chosen for the book, she might just as well have been talking about herself: ". . . all, without exception, are creative and warmhearted human beings with a sense of the romantic possibilities, as well as the practical demands, of everyday existence."

This Regency bowfront bookcase displays my collection of porcelain fruits and vegetables made by Lady Anne Gordon, Mary Kirk Kelly, and Katherine Houston. The single asparagus on the bottom shelf was given to me by my staff. The turnip reminds me of growing up in the South. On top of the bookcase is a more traditional arrangement: a pair of unusual nineteenth-century candlesticks, two English porcelain urns, a cabbage from Anne Gordon, and a lamp made from a gilded architectural ornament.

On an English marble-top table in the living room, parrots by Lady Anne Gordon guard a lunch of apricots, pineapple, and limes made of marble, ivory, and porcelain. The decalcomania lamp sports cutouts of animals and tropical plants. On the stippled wall, the theme is echoed by deft Chinese paintings of fruits, flowers, and insects.

Asked if she believed in creating a mood in the home, decorator Dorothy Draper replied, "No one is constantly in the same mood; if there is to be a set mood, I'm usually for gaiety with restraint and always for a basis of solid comfort."

133

A starburst Italian barometer is but one of the cast of characters that populates this lively mantel. Treasured blue-and-white porcelains are symmetrically arranged on either side of the mirror. The mirror's nineteenth-century Spanish frame is made of gesso and silver gilt, its original glass reflecting the room and the porcelain collection on the opposite wall as well. The dining table is pulled snugly up to the fire. Its centerpiece: a miniature hand-painted wheelbarrow loaded with a flourishing Boston fern. Two pair of creamware candlesticks with paper pleated shades guard the fern at either end. A hearth broom stands to one side of the mantel, ready to whisk flying sparks back into the fire.

A mantel is often an easel reflecting the passions of the people who live in the house. On this mantel, the mirror is a place to tuck photographs, and favorite postcards from friends. Blue and white delftware sets off a brass basket bearing apples. The silver-based candle globes intensify the twinkle of candlelight by night.

The desire for symmetry, for balance, for rhythm is one of the most inveterate of human instincts.
Edith Wharton and Ogden Codman, Jr.

This salt-glazed Wedgwood teapot, with its King Charles spaniel top, recalls the delicacy of ivory miniatures.

Photograph on opposite page

Who wouldn't want to settle in for an evening of reading, in a restful bedroom like this one? On the bedside table, a faux bois papier-mâché bucket of full-blown roses sets an atmosphere of beauty and calm. Pencils in a satyr's pot are poised for action when middle-of-the-night inspirations occur. The gathering of favorite photographs framed in alligator, monogrammed leather, silver, and brass are a mix of old and new. A frail Gothic chair holds only books these days. The antique needlepoint rug with violets spreads a garden underfoot.

A collection of spaniels turns this hallway corner into a tiny gallery. Parian ware, bronze, and porcelain spaniels recline on the table-top, while nineteenth- and twentieth-century engravings, sketches, and paintings cover the wall. The magnificent tole clock was handmade in Paris by Clare Mosley. A glossy black shade caps the brass Directoire-style lamp and casts a subtle glow in this corner.

In the dining room, a table-top assemblage of curious small silver objects aptly expresses the owner's varied interests and her lively sense of humor. The collection has grown little by little, year by year.

This needlepoint pillow playfully points up everyone's favorite fantasy.

T he living room's scagliola table decorated with a ring of trailing vines circles a fragrant gardenia in an ordinary clay pot. Awaiting company are a pair of pottery twig chairs, sized for Papa Bear and Baby Bear, or their equivalents. The ebony and ivory frame shows the property's guest cottage; the photograph was taken on the day the house was purchased.

VITA SACKVILLE-WEST

1892–1962

Victoria Mary Sackville-West was perhaps better known to the masses as a gardener than an author and poet because of a popular gardening column she wrote for an English newspaper.

She and her husband, Sir Harold Nicholson, turned a ramshackle conglomerate of disparate buildings into the incomparable Sissinghurst Castle, where they lived with their two sons.

She liked messiness; he liked tidiness. Together, they created one of the most famous gardens in England, one that has been copied by passionate gardeners all over the world. He built the straight paths; she planted with abandon the herbs and bushes, and the "brown flowers" her husband said she preferred, which flowed out into his paths and sight lines.

In all she did, we can assume that Sackville-West held fast to one of her favorite gardening maxims. "Hoick it out!" she would exclaim, about anything out of place or mischosen.

When she worked, Vita retreated to her writing table in the Elizabethan Tower. Her "Tower Room" was a first-floor office in a building separate from the main house. It was her sanctuary; her own son says he stepped into the place only three or four times during his growing-up years, so sanctified and private was the feeling of the place.

The room has been preserved much as it was in Vita's day, and one can see the treasured books, family photographs, and the cherished tapestry on the wall.

*I'm a great believer in vulgarity—
if it's got vitality. A little bad taste
is like a nice splash of paprika. We
all need a splash of bad taste—
it's hearty, it's healthy, it's physi-
cal. I think we could use more of it.
No taste is what I'm against.*

Diana Vreeland, *DV*

Porcelain plates of pretend vegetables march across this dining room mantel, giving lighthearted approval to feasting of any sort. At night, crystal sconces set the room to twinkling. Red walls are a soft accompaniment.

The gherkins are phony, but it's hard to tell, especially when the ladybugs have joined the picnic.

It's hard to believe this indoor playroom has no windows. The perennial border is always blooming, the animals are always ambling along the garden path, and the country landscape beckons beyond. All this, thanks to the skillful fool-the-eye painting of artist James Arkin Smith. The latticework entrance to the play area was adapted from a 1920s English gardening book. The lattice on the wall was incorporated into the painting to mirror the architectural detail.

After digging up the garden (and then reading about it!), this hand-carved retriever helps himself to a well-deserved rest.

The surprises in my sisal-matted foyer are the stone ornaments and containers that I've brought inside from the garden. Under an English giltwood table decorated with acorns and oak leaves lies a stone basket overflowing with a fragrant mix of potpourri, dried flowers, and pine cones. The stone tulip pot bears a hardy green plant. The squirrel is just a friendly visitor.

The selective eye must be an experienced eye, an eye that knows the genuine pleasures of harmonious colors and textures, of sensitive line and proportion, of the play in contrasts of light and shade. The selective eye must see beyond immediate limitations, recognize possibilities that a fertile imagination suggests, and translate the difference between the genuine and the false. The selective eye must also be quick to respond to those things, tangible or intangible, that are the elusive—perhaps even witty—ingredients of a happy room.

Mrs. Eleanor Brown, *Finest Rooms*

In the sunroom, faux stone walls and a matching floor are host to a passel of trompe l'oeil tree frogs out for an afternoon of rock climbing.

Shelves are another kind of artist's canvas: a place for display that will capture the eye. This niche harbors an antique Noah's Ark and all the hand-carved animals marching two by two. The other shelves bear shapely teapots, platters, and plates, most with a floral motif.

Photograph on opposite page

Clare Potter describes the object on her painted satinwood table as "a tapestry of our life." There's a memory, a place, a friend, or a story attached to each one. What could be more personal? The table belonged to her husband Nick's grandmother. A miniature shoe is tossed on its side, as if lost by Cinderella in her race against the clock. In fact, two of her horses have turned back into mice and hide nearby. The casual position of the shoe gives this arrangement an active feeling, as opposed to a stiff, passive one. The distinction is subtle, yet potent!

No matter what the weather is outside, my guests always have blue skies in their bathroom! The walls were painted by artist Anne Harris, who dotted the "sky" with birds and vines. A leafy double-candle sconce, painted green, continues the illusion. Lampshades are made of a coordinating silk.

Miniature Windsor chairs perch on the mantel as if awaiting tiny visitors.

To give an indoor room the feeling of outdoors, bring on the flora and fauna! In this playroom, flowers bloom on walls and window shades, and wooden animals peer out from their perches. A real brick wall is covered with lattice, which also disguises the radiator. Wooden lanterns and outdoor garden furniture complete the fantasy.

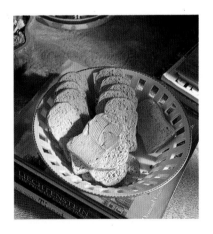

The ants have made a picnic of this basket of buttered bread, and only taste will tell you whether it's real or not. In fact, this porcelain basket with ceramic trompe l'oeil bread, the work of a French artist with a wonderful sense of humor, causes everyone to do a double take.

149

V

AT

HOME

. . . a true home . . . is not defined by its likeness

to other houses of similar or superior social standing,

but rather by its individuality expressed

in unpretentious honesty; its contents,

that is, are determined by the affections, not by

conformity to an agreed standard of "taste."

Philippa Tristam, *Living Space*

WHENEVER I READ A DECORATING book, I'm curious about how the author really lives. So this chapter is about "Chez Charlotte," as my friends have dubbed my house.

I live here with my husband, two sons, and two spaniels, Woody and Chequers, and we all feel mighty comfortable here. It seems we all have our favorite places to retreat to for private time. My husband gravitates toward his library. I

We welcome you most cordially.
We welcome you most regally . . .
Mayor of Munchkinland to Dorothy and
Toto, *The Wizard of Oz*

Photograph on previous page

favor the reading chaise in our bedroom, and the kids hunker down in their rooms or convene en masse with friends on the long, friendly banquette in our breakfast room (yes, there's a picture of this in the book—we just cleared away the pizza boxes!).

It's a treat—and a trial—to give shape to a space that's just waiting for your touch. In decorating, the eternal question always is, "So what should I do with this?"

Entryways are intriguing and often curious little spaces ripe with possibilities. Here in the entry to my own home, an elevator landing in a New York apartment building, a Danish trompe l'oeil table from the early nineteenth century is paired with an Irish Regency mirror. Inlaid faceted glass along the mirror's edge catches the light from all angles. On either side of the mirror are eighteenth-century engravings of French fables by Oudry. A pair of painted and gold-leafed brackets support blue-and-white vases and plates. To give the space architecture and a feeling consistent with the rest of the house, I added dentiled molding, door surrounds, and a pediment above the door. The walls were painted to simulate stone; the painted faux bois technique utilized on the molding creates the look of aged burled wood. Overhead, a tole lantern sheds a soft welcoming glow. The flowers and their containers change constantly. The floor is marble and indestructible.

I have very strong feelings about this sort of space. When you live in a vertical city like New York you encounter lots of elevator halls in the period of a week. So many of them are neglected, boring, out of date, and depressing that I cannot imagine beginning and ending my day passing through them. When I leave my house I can't wait to get back to it, and, when I do, I want it to say "Hey—welcome home!"

Before we moved in, I spent countless hours just walking through the rooms of this apartment, letting the ideas percolate . . . always, always, with my proverbial notebook in hand. I measured, I sketched, and I imagined.

In any new room, you want to let the house talk to you before you begin imposing your ideas on it. After all, what living space doesn't come with its own history and set of standards, whether the construction be old or new. You must listen to the walls, talk to the cupboards, hear what the floorboards say. Mumbo-jumbo? Maybe. But it's part of the language of any house, and this apartment was no exception. I put my ear to the ground.

There was a stateliness to this apartment that spoke to me immediately. The prewar building itself has an air of quiet elegance that I wanted to be true to. Upstairs, on the seventh floor, a loftier feeling prevailed.

Step by step, my decorating plan began to take shape. I say plan, but in the opening stages, my plan was more of a montage in my mind. I saw a painting here, a secretaire there, our bed in the master bedroom, and even envisioned what fabric would look good in the guest bath.

Then the real work began. When I decorate, I'm always meticulous about documenting everything that must be done: the hows, whys, and wherefores. I began a notebook for each room, and kept all the appropriate swatches, paint samples, and resources in enve-

The house is but the externalized man.

Frank A. Parsons, *Interior Decoration: Its Principles and Practice*

lopes inside. Sometimes at night I would pick one room, spread out all the samples and whatnot, and juggle them around, extracting, replacing, trying this and that.

I treated myself as one of my own clients when the project began, allocating—or trying to allocate—the same amount of time and energy to this project as to any of my other clients. Otherwise something this massive just doesn't get done.

Of course, a house is never finished, but at least we got the basics in place. And now, each day we live here, the house and our family become closer friends.

Well, now that those preliminaries are out of the way, I'd like to show you my house.

If you were actually standing on my threshold, I'd greet you at the door, take your coat, then settle you into the most comfortable chair. After offering you a cup of tea I'd take you on a tour of the house.

"To express the things of the spirit in visible form": it's my belief that our spirits are most honestly expressed not by sofas, curtains, and carpets, but by the stack of favorite mysteries or gardening books on a side table, flowers on the windowsill, or porcelains displayed in the dining room. These "telling details"—our objects, bibelots, whatnots, and knickknacks—say the most about who we are. They are as honest as a diary.

Your things create a mood, a spirit, an atmosphere that's unmistakably you. As Billy Baldwin once said, "What we remember

Hollyhocks are one of my favorite cottage garden flowers, so it's not surprising that my living room mantel is graced by a pair of hand-sculpted and -painted clay hollyhocks. These were made especially for me by New York artist Clare Potter for a room I decorated one summer at the Southampton Decorator Showhouse. The early nineteenth-century Derby plates were chosen for their classical appeal. The mantel garniture is English porcelain; I can't resist buying these pieces for myself and for my shop. They are pretty just to look at, and even prettier filled with flowers. An Adam border glass mirror reflects the room.

most about rooms we like is the 'atmosphere.' " He felt this atmosphere could be achieved only through "enormous personal manifestation." In other words, by showing your own stuff!

Exaggerating ideas and concepts without inhibitions, dropping the reins of your imagination, indulging your fantasies, investigating with your eyes, keeping an open mind, and ad-libbing—these are the seeds of creation.

When it comes to decorating, try to forget what you have seen before and what you have been told should or should not be done. You will have more fun in the process, and will derive much more pleasure from the results if you allow yourself to "start from scratch."

Simultaneously, you must get excited about your ideas, about your "project." Decorating fashions and trends are to be observed, analyzed, and appreciated—not blindly followed. In other words, do only what works for you.

So take a moment to roam slowly through your house, room by room. Look around and ask yourself, "Is this me?"

If the answer is yes, you can relax and assume that your personal style will be heard, like a gentle whisper.

If the answer is no, then it's time to get to work. Go through your house and "edit" carefully and thoughtfully. Take out what is wrong for you. Rearrange. Move items from room to room. Don't forget to look in closets, drawers, and attics for those things you may have forgotten.

Vita Sackville-West had a single philosophy about the things in her garden that did not work. "Hoick it out!" she said. Vita's husband, Harold Nicolson, described her style as "ruthless."

Be just as ruthless with your house. Vita's basic gardening principle is just as useful indoors as outdoors. After all, a house is organic, too!

All my life I have been plagued by a passion for detail. I have a vision of how I want certain things done. I am sure I drive my staff crazy, just as I drove my mother crazy when I used to rearrange the living room time and again. Lucky for me Mom was patient, and for some reason she trusted me.

In my shop, I have specified how packages should be wrapped, how customers are to be greeted, even what flowers are on the *never* list.

At home, I have a similar code. Certain linens go with certain china patterns. And I am constantly adjusting tabletop arrangements to get them just right—at least, just right for me.

We must occasionally remind ourselves of our brief visit on this planet. Shouldn't we try to express ourselves clearly, make a personal stamp on our environment, and pay attention to the details that make the difference?

In planning and decorating the dining room my goal was to evoke a little romance. An antique Russian crystal chandelier sparkling overhead, the red walls painstakingly stenciled, and the mirrored sconces all seem to communicate, especially at night when the lights are on. The breakfront is filled with an assortment of silver, crystal, and botanical porcelain collected from family, auctions and antiquing excursions. On the table, a pair of silver candlesticks watch carefully over a silver tureen overflowing with variegated hydrangeas.

Because breakfast is generally taken in the breakfast room and lunch is almost always at my desk, this room receives most of its attention at night. It is large but it is cozy, it is dark yet it is warm. Sometimes I just sit at the end of the table nearest the window, have some tea, and write a few letters—it gives me another excuse to be there.

Have nothing in your homes that you do not know to be useful and believe to be beautiful.
William Morris

I love silver! As a group, it creates a glittering landscape, while a single piece makes a quiet statement. On the Regency sideboard in my dining room, you'll find everything from intricately tooled Victorian silver to the refined lines of Georgian pieces. The urn is my favorite shape; I like to fill the urns with fruit, flowers, or both!

The breakfast room of our house is a favorite family gathering place. It was originally a maid's dining room. We eliminated the wall that divided it from the kitchen and created a place to cook, to eat, and to chat. The dogs nap on the banquette, my youngest stepson and his buddies devour pizza here, and on Sundays the place is covered with the *New York Times*. A large German painting of sheep grazing at dusk dominates the space. The other wall is decorated with eighteenth-century paintings and watercolors of cows and landscapes.

Walls of duck-egg blue are warmed by a chintz that's primarily cream, deep red, and shades of brown. On the deep windowsill sits an antique tole cachepot filled with greenery and a pair of early nineteenth-century English salt-glaze plates. Supervising all the action from overhead is a double-tiered tole chandelier.

This room is a synthesis of our family lifestyle. We are casual, and we crave comfort. We love color—as long as it doesn't shout. We love animals, whether canvas or real. My one bit of license was the bullion on the balloon shades. Somehow it was like putting a period at the end of a sentence.

Photograph on opposite page

Watercolors and pastels of interiors add a fourth dimension to my living room, where flowers and garden colors are the theme. In one corner, a chintz-draped table is topped by a Paris porcelain lamp decorated with intricately painted flowers. The silver bowl, modeled to look like leaves, cradles a fragrant mix of potpourri, dried roses, hollyhocks, and delphinium. The flowers were preserved by drying them in silica gel. Tucked away atop the tomes is a majestic stone lion; lions are a favorite of mine, and you'll find them all around my house.

Things that are especially dear to me seem to gravitate to the sofa table in my living room. Family photographs are displayed in silver frames. My miniature Victorian silver watering can tends the needs of the blue clay auricula given to me by my office staff for Christmas. The silver wishbone tongs were a present from Anne Harris, who did all the murals and decorative painting in my house. My housekeeper, Valerie, brought the miniature silver urn back from one of her visits to Ireland.

On my dressing table, an eighteenth-century miniature of a young girl painted on ivory. I like the contrast of her innocent face and the incredible detail and sophistication of the bronze doré frame.

Beauty is the quality of harmoni-ous relationships. A formula to produce if it does not exist.

Frank A. Parsons, *Interior Decoration: Its Principles and Practice*

Photograph on opposite page

Life imitates art in my guest room, where a watercolor depicts old-fashioned roses and lavender tumbling from a basket. You can close your eyes and imagine Provence.

Pictures have a way of setting a tone in a room, and this corner of my husband's library is a good example. A painting of the Hudson River is a serene focal point, flanked by four eighteenth-century Dutch engravings of birds.

The pillows on the velvet sofa were arranged with similar care, the armorial needlepoint resting on a trio of nineteenth-century paisleys. A stand was specially made for the coffee table, which is really a scenic French tole tray.

A simple Parsons table covered with two layers of fabric provides a place to jot a note. The bows at each corner give this table a fully dressed look, the clutter of invitations and cards invites a curious browser.

Fully aware of its ability to capture attention from any angle, I gave this Dutch still life center stage in my living room. The painting is hung between lushly draped windows (their valances echo the painting's crowning motif), a pair of French bergères covered in a bold plaid, and two architectural table lamps. The welcoming arms of the silk damask sofa bear some of my favorite treasures: antique silk Beauvais tapestry pillows. The black nineteenth-century lacquered chinoiserie tray, which I had made into a table, provides the punctuation in this colorful group. I use black a lot in this way; it provides a spark or crucial contrast.

SOURCEBOOK

There are so many wonderful shops around the country that I could have written a book just listing them. But what I have done here is give you the highlights, those special places that are always on my list whenever I am traveling. You will not be disappointed if you visit any of them.

Evans and Gerst Antiques
3500 East Fourth Street
Long Beach, CA 90814
(213) 439-1404

Eclectic and sophisticated: Their specialty is English, Irish, and Continental furniture of the eighteenth and nineteenth centuries, with painted and lacquered finishes. They also have all kinds of tole, porcelain, and garden items. The shop is favored by many West Coast designers.

Hollyhock
214 North Larchmont Boulevard
Los Angeles, CA 90004
(213) 931-3400

Hollyhock is London in California: a decorating store chock-full of delicious necessities and indulgences for house and garden. They have their own down-filled upholstered chairs and sofas copied from old pieces, and an assortment of antique furniture to complement them. Always in stock are black Victorian papier-mâché ebonized and lacquered pieces, a large selection of pillows—needlepoint, chintz, and painted silk—unusual lamps, and English, French, and Chinese porcelain. Painted tole cachepots and old watering cans, painted and papered boxes, painted furniture, and English hand-thrown pots are also found here. Their specialty is botanical watercolors, mainly from the Regency and Victorian periods. All this is displayed in a homelike setting that includes a bright, open patio for Regency wirework garden furniture and decorations.

Indigo Seas
123 North Robertson Boulevard
Los Angeles, CA 90048
(213) 550-8758

Walking into this shop is like entering a gentleman planter's island retreat: The floor at the entrance is painted with a map of the Caribbean, leading in to a treasure trove of antique wicker chairs, upholstered furniture slipcovered in old chintz and faded printed linens from the twenties. Scottish cashmeres in Bermuda colors, silver tea sets, kilim rugs and old veranda furniture are all displayed with a dash of whimsy.

Thomas M. Beeton, Inc.
930½ North La Cienega Boulevard
Los Angeles, CA 90069
(213) 657-1371

Original painted finishes and surfaces are a specialty, and decorative furniture and objects of the seventeenth, eighteenth, and mid-nineteenth centuries mix and mingle happily.

Ireland-Pays
2428 Main Street
Santa Monica, CA 90405
(213) 396-5035

This boutique, co-owned by actress Amanda Pays and model Kathy Ireland, is filled with antique furniture and reproductions from France and England.

G. R. Durenberger Inc.
31531 Camino Capistrano
San Juan Capistrano, CA 92675
(714) 493-1283

In an old building with a garden and a fountain, this shop showcases primarily late eighteenth- and early nineteenth-century English and French antiques.

Norman Shepherd
458 Jackson Street
San Francisco, CA 94111
(415) 362-4145

Montauk Highway
Water Mill, NY 11976
(516) 726-4840

If San Francisco isn't close by, maybe Norman Shepherd's shop in Water Mill, New York, is. The warm atmosphere here translates from coast to coast. There's an elegant mix of antique English, French, and European furniture, primarily from the seventeenth, eighteenth, and nineteenth centuries. He also sells beautiful Chinese porcelains. Because there are always some interesting Arts and Crafts items to be had, Norman Shepherd has become an important resource for anyone decorating in this style.

Bell 'Ochio
8 Brady Street
San Francisco, CA 94103
(415) 864-4048

Owners Claudia Schwartz and Toby Hanson certainly have "an eye for the beauti-ful"—the translation of the shop's name. A small store that belongs to a different era, it beckons you to linger and inspect its stock of hand-dyed ribbons, imported handmade silk nosegays, fragrances, note cards, and decorative treasures.

Jeffrey Davies
575 Sutter Street
San Francisco, CA 94103
(415) 392-1722

A large inviting showroom full of Continental antiques and accessories plus an amazing assortment of the most lifelike silk flowers from France.

Sue Fisher King
3067 Sacramento Street
San Francisco, CA 94115
(415) 922-7276

Bed, bath and table linens imported from Italy and France. You'll also find a wonderful array of decorative accessories.

Anthony P. Browne
2903 M Street N.W.
Washington, DC 20007
(202) 333-1903

This walk-in design shop offers fabrics and furnishings of a style and quality not usually available to the retail customer.

Janis Aldridge, Inc.
2900 M Street
Washington, DC 20007
(202) 338-7710

7 Center Street
Nantucket, MA 02554
(508) 228-6673

8452 Melrose Place
Los Angeles, CA 90069
(213) 658-8456

The walls are lined with matted and framed botanical prints that span four centuries, which evokes the feeling of being in an indoor garden. In addition to the botanicals, the shop features decorative accessories, choice porcelains, and prints of architectural and interior views.

Lori Ponder
5221 Wisconsin Avenue N.W.
Washington, DC 20015
(202) 537-1010

Decorating? Looking for a great gift? Displayed in inviting room settings, Lori's stock is a treasure trove of antique boxes, pillows, lamps, cachepots, and porcelains.

Rooms and Gardens
1675 Wisconsin Avenue N.W.
Washington, DC 20007
(202) 965-3820

"A celebration of the threshold between indoor living and outdoor living." The creative displays of this innovative design shop make you realize that even an outdoor garden bench can look marvelous in an entrance hall. Pictures, topiaries, glassware, local crafts and choice European treasures. Owner Margaret Rubino, cutting tree branches instead of fresh flowers, fills the shop with an abundance of greens that give Rooms and Gardens an outdoorsy fragrance.

The Ashley Gallery
9A Via Parigi
Palm Beach, FL 33480
(305) 659-5150

If you love eighteenth- and nineteenth-century English and Irish furniture and paintings, The Ashley Gallery should be in your "Palm Beach to Do" file. They have a lovely selection of papier-mâché and treen, and many different collections in miniature, including porcelain tea and dinner services, tables, and chests of drawers. They also carry a variety of Georgian and Regency cut glass, decanters, wineglasses, and finger bowls—one of my weaknesses. Their furniture includes good Georgian chests and tea tables, Regency mahogany hanging shelves and sideboards, and Adam carved pine chimney pieces. Paintings are mainly of a sporting nature, plus landscapes and some unusual Regency needlework pictures. Sheila Potter découpage lamps are always available and can be made to order.

Mary Mahoney
340 Worth Avenue
Palm Beach, FL 33480
(407) 655-5751

Mary Mahoney offers the finest in luxury home furnishings and gift items, from

D. Porthault in the bedroom to Flora Danica in the dining room.

The Summerhouse
319 Worth Avenue
Palm Beach, FL 33480
(407) 659-6036

The Summerhouse is a source for an eclectic mix of antiques, fine reproduction accessories and home furnishings.

The Country French Connection
575 East Wesley Road
Atlanta, GA 30305
(404) 237-4907

Porthault linens, trompe l'oeil furniture and fire screens, porcelain reproductions, and earthenware fruits. You'll also find vases and brackets, mirrors, screens, and fragrance, plus French antique furniture and reproductions.

Branca, Inc.
65 West Illinois Street
Chicago, IL 60610
(312) 822-0751

In Chicago, Branca is the place for hand-decorated matting and framing, painted finishes, antique furniture, prints, and all kinds of wonderful accessories. Their hand-painted silk pillows, painted furniture, folding screens, tables, boxes, lamps, and lampshades are all beautiful and irresistible. Everything can be custom-made to your specifications, in your own particular colors and prints.

American Country Store
57 Main Street
East Hampton, NY 11937
(516) 324-2276

The American Country Store specializes in folk art, garden accessories, Christmas items, and a large array of country antiques for the home.

English Country Antiques
Snake Hollow Road
Bridgehampton, NY 11932
(516) 537-0606

Owned by photographer Chris Meade, this huge store is filled with pine furniture, English china, bed and table linens, and lots of lamps—you can furnish your house with one stop.

Victory Garden
63 Main Street
East Hampton, NY 11937
(516) 324-7800

The Mediterranean flavor of Victory Garden is apparent the minute one steps into the shop: giant olive jars from Provence, antique garden ornaments, dried flower arrangements, Italian lamps and sconces.

Lee Bogart
250 Birch Hill Road
Locust Valley, NY 11560

Reminiscent of an English decorating shop, Lee Bogart is filled with wings of fabrics and wallpaper books as well as antiques, and offers interior design services.

Valley House Antiques
182 Birch Hill Road
Locust Valley, NY 11560
(516) 671-2847

Decorative furniture and accessories are displayed in four furnished rooms of a charming old house.

Charlotte Moss & Co.
1027 Lexington Avenue
New York, NY 10021
(212) 772-3320

Of course, my own shop is one of my favorite haunts. And yes, you'll often find me there—a shopkeeper tending shop. I stock all the things I think a wonderful home should have. It's a small shop, lined with tall bookcases displaying a cozy clutter of treasures, including porcelains, lamps and lamp shades in all shapes and colors, silver, painted furniture, needlepoint-design rugs, painted tole and papier-mâché, scented candles, antique tapestry and chintz pillows, my collection of upholstered furniture, and books.

Cherchez
862 Lexington Avenue
New York, NY 10021
(212) 737-8215

China, new and antique bed linens, small antique treasures and pretty ribbons are among the stock at Cherchez. All of owner Barbara Ohrbach's books can be found nestled amongst paisley shawls and pillows and large boxes of potpourri.

Dampierre & Co.
79 Greene Street
New York, NY 10012
(212) 966-5474

In her converted Soho warehouse, Florence de Dampiere has gathered a vast collection of Italian and French fabrics, handpainted faux bois china, furniture from Patina, and a wonderful selection of painted nineteenth-century antiques. The case for painted furniture is made here. Be sure to pick up copies of her books, **The Decorator** *and* **The Best of Painted Furniture.**

John Rosselli
255 East 72nd Street
New York, NY 10021
(212) 772-2137

Antiques and decorations, faux finishes on custom reproductions.

Lexington Gardens
1008 Lexington Avenue
New York, NY 10021
(212) 861-4390

Decorative accessories for the garden and other objects with the garden theme.

Zona
97 Greene Street
New York, NY 10012
(212) 925-6750

Tucked away in Soho, Zona is curiously cozy despite its large floor space and very high ceilings. Handcrafts from the U.S. and abroad line the walls and shelves here. Everything from hand-milled soaps to textiles to furniture and select, one-of-a-kind items delight every sense.

planters, and the one-of-a-kind something you can't do without. Richard has a great eye and uses it to cherry-pick great items for his shop.

Circa
2321 Crescent Avenue
Charlotte, NC 28207
(704) 332-1668

Don't go to Charlotte without visiting the Circa shop. I love all their one-of-a-kind European antiques, Majolica, Staffordshire, Imari, and Rose Medallion. They have a huge selection of designer fabrics and wallpaper, plus a custom upholstery service. Circa is well known in the Southeast for its personal, unique look and friendly atmosphere. It makes you feel at home.

Mary Anne
410 Libbie Avenue
Richmond, VA 23226
(804) 282-4141

English country with a Virginia accent on Mary Anne's hand-picked inventory of painted and upholstered furniture and accessories makes instant decorating possible. If your needs are more extensive, she can decorate for you too.

R. Kazarian Antiques
35 Franklin Street
Newport, RI 02840
(401) 846-3563

The European and American painted furniture here tends to be in "as found" condition—take it or leave it—and I've unearthed some great finds here. They also carry an interesting assemblage of architectural fragments and garden details such as lead and stone ornaments, iron benches,

Robert Blair Antiques Ltd.
5605 Grove Avenue
Richmond, VA 23226

In a townhouse setting where the air smells like boxwood, eighteenth- and nineteenth-century English furniture, delicious porcelain, and a mix of antique cushions and decorative objects are served up with the finest Southern hospitality. There are plenty of choice paintings—animal motifs are particular favorites here. Best of all, they'll deliver, hang your pictures, put your china in your breakfront. Who could ask for anything more?

BIBLIOGRAPHY

Aakre, Nancy. *L'Art de Vivre. Decorative Arts & Design in France, 1789–1989*. New York: Vendome Press, Cooper-Hewitt Museum, 1989.

Adams, William Howard. *Jefferson's Monticello*. New York: Abbeville Press, 1983.

Baldwin, Billy. *Billy Baldwin Decorates*. Secaucus, N.J.: Chartwell Books, 1972.

Beaton, Cecil. *Ashcombe: The Story of a Fifteen-Year Lease*. London: B. T. Batsford Ltd., 1949.

———. *The Glass of Fashion*. Garden City, N.Y.: Doubleday & Co., 1954.

Buchan, Ursula, ed. *A Bouquet of Garden Writing*. Boston: David R. Godine, 1987.

Carter, Ernestine. "Style," 1976 in *The Vogue Bedside Reader,* edited by Josephine Ross. London: Vermilion, 1984.

Charles-Roux, Edmonde. *Chanel*. New York: Alfred A. Knopf, 1975.

Cooke, Lawrence S. *Lighting in America*. Pittstown, N.J.: Main Street Press, 1984.

Coward, Noel. *Play Parade*. Garden City, N.Y.: Doubleday & Co., 1951.

de Maupassant, Guy. *Pierre and Jean*. New York: Penguin Books, 1979.

Devonshire, Duchess of. *The House: A Portrait of Chatsworth*. London: Macmillan, 1982.

de Wolfe, Elsie. *After All*. New York: Harper & Brothers, 1935.

———. *The House in Good Taste*. New York: Century Company, 1914.

Ellmann, Richard. *Oscar Wilde, A Collection of Critical Essays*. New York: Prentice Hall, 1969.

Faude, Wilson H. *The Renaissance of Mark Twain's House: Handbook for Restoration*. Larchmont, N.Y.: Queens House, 1978.

Fleischmann, Melanie. *In the Neoclassic Style*. London: Columbus Books, Ltd., 1988/ New York: Thames & Hudson, 1988.

Fowler, John, and John Cornforth. *English Decoration in the Eighteenth Century,* 2d ed. London: Barrie & Jenkins, 1974.

Gardine, Michael. *Billy Baldwin, An Autobiography*. Boston: Little, Brown and Co., 1985.

Guild, Tricia, and Elizabeth Wilhide. *Tricia Guild's Design and Detail*. London: Conran Octopus Ltd., 1988/New York: Simon & Schuster, 1988.

Guild, Robin. *The Finishing Touch*. London: Marshall Editions Ltd., 1979.

Hibberd, Shirley. *Rustic Adornments for Homes of Taste*. London: Century Hutchinson Ltd., 1987. (First pub. 1856.)

Hicks, David. *Living With Design*. London: Weidenfeld & Nicolson Ltd., 1979.

Hog, Min and others. *Interiors*. New York: Clarkson N. Potter, 1988.

John, Augustus. "Interior Decoration," 1928 in *The Vogue Bedside Reader,* edited by Josephine Ross. London: Vermilion, 1984.

Johnson, Lorraine, and Gabrielle Townsend. *Osborne & Little: The Decorated Room*. Woodstock, N.Y.: Overlook Press, 1988.

Kennett, Frances. *Coco: The Life and Loves of Gabrielle Chanel*. London: Victor Gollancz Ltd., 1989.

Kornfeld, Albert. *The Doubleday Book of Interior Decorating*. Garden City, N.Y.: Doubleday & Co., 1965.

Koves, Helen. *On Decorating the House*. New York: Cosmopolitan Book Corp., 1928.

Kron, Joan. *Home-Psych*. New York: Clarkson N. Potter, 1983.

Lockwood, Sarah M. *Decoration: Past, Present, and Future*. Garden City, N.Y.: Doubleday, Doran & Co., 1935.

Lisle, Laurie. *Portrait of an Artist: A Biography of Georgia O'Keeffe*. New York: Washington Square Press, 1987.

Lynes, Russell. *The Tastemakers: The Shaping of American Popular Taste*. New York: Dover Publications, 1949.

McLaughlin, Jack. *Jefferson & Monticello, The Biography of a Builder*. New York: Henry Holt, 1988.

Manchester, William. *The Last Lion, Winston Spencer Churchill, Alone, 1932–1940*. Boston: Little, Brown and Co., 1988.

Masters, Brian. *Great Hostesses*. London: Constable & Co., 1982.

Metcalf, Pauline, ed. *Ogden Codman and the Decoration of Houses.* Boston: Boston Athenaeum, 1988.

Miller, Gladys. *Decoratively Speaking.* Garden City, N.Y.: Doubleday, Doran & Co., 1939.

National Trust Studies. *Writers at Home.* London: Trefoil Books, 1985.

Osborne, Harold, ed. *The Oxford Companion to the Decorative Arts.* New York: Oxford University Press, 1985.

Page, Russell. *The Education of a Gardener,* rev. ed. Middlesex, England: Penguin Books, 1985.

Pahlmann, William. *The Pahlmann Book of Interior Design.* New York: Thomas Crowell & Co., 1955.

Parsons, Frank A. *Interior Decoration: Its Principles and Practice.* New York: Doubleday Page & Co., 1915.

Phillips, Barty. *The Country House Book.* London: Ebury Press, 1988.

Post, Emily. *The Personality of the House.* New York: Funk & Wagnalls, 1930.

Robinson, William. *The English Flower Garden.* New York: Amaryllis Press, 1984.

Rybczynski, Witold. *Home. A Short History of an Idea.* New York: Viking Penguin, 1986.

Sackville-West, Vita. *English Country Houses.* London: William Collins, 1942.

Tankard, Judith, and Michael R. Van Vackenburgh. *Gertrude Jekyll, A Vision of Garden and Wood.* New York: Harry Abrams, 1988.

Tristam, Philippa. *Living Space.* London: Routledge, 1989.

Trollope, Frances. *Domestic Manners of the Americans,* rev. ed. London: Century Publishing Company, 1984. (First pub. London: Bentley, 1839.)

Tweed, Katharine, ed. *The Finest Rooms by America's Great Decorators.* New York: Viking Press, 1964.

Vickers, Hugo. *Cecil Beaton.* London: Weidenfeld & Nicolson, 1985.

Wharton, Edith, and Ogden Codman, Jr. *The Decoration of Houses.* New York: W. W. Norton, 1978.